The
Urban
Loft

The Urban Loft

Creating a Dream Space in the City

MARTIN MYERS

Fitzhenry & Whiteside

The Urban Loft
Copyright © 2005 Martin Myers

In Canada:
Fitzhenry and Whiteside Limited
195 Allstate Parkway
Markham, Ontario L3R 4T8

In the United States:
121 Harvard Avenue, Suite 2
Allston, Massachusetts 02134

www.fitzhenry.ca godwit@fitzhenry.ca

Fitzhenry & Whiteside acknowledges with thanks the Canada Council for the Arts, the Government of Canada through its Book Publishing Industry Development Program, and the Ontario Arts Council for their support of our publishing program.

10 9 8 7 6 5 4 3 2 1

Library and Archives Canada Cataloguing in Publication
Myers, Martin
The urban loft : creating a dream space in the city / Martin Myers.
ISBN 1-55041-839-4
1. Lofts—Remodeling for other use—Anecdotes. I. Title.
NA7882.M84 2005   643'.5   C2005-903858-3

United States Publisher Cataloging-in-Publication Data
Myers, Martin.
The urban loft : creating a dream space in the city / Martin Myers.—1st ed. [256] p. : ill. ; cm.
Summary: An instructive and humorous record of one couple's search and creation of an urban loft space in a major city
ISBN 1-55041-839-4
1. Lofts. 2. Lofts — Remodeling for other use.
I. Title.
747 dc22 TH3000.M947 2005

Designed by Kerry Designs
Front cover image and photographs on pages 52, 93, 104 and 106 by Linda Corbett of Eyeris Interactive Inc.
Photographs on pages XI, XII, 39, 41, 43, 49, 50, 51, 63, 64, 66, 67, 68, 70, 81, 111, 112 and 114 by
Colleen Dagnall of Colleen Dagnall Photography. All other photographs by Colleen Myers.

Spaces engender thought.
— Richard Serra, sculptor

Our house . . . is our first universe, a real cosmos in every sense of the word.
— Gaston Bachelard, philosopher, *The Poetics of Space*

The spaces we live in colour our lives. They are our lives.
— Inmate 845921, Gormley Penal Institution

Fiction by Martin Myers
The Assignment
Frigate
Izzy Manheim's Reunion

CONTENTS

PART II

CHALLENGING TRANSITIONS

PART III

OUR FINISHED ACQUISITION

Introduction

This book deals briefly with all the residential spaces I have lived in, from the cramped, rented flat of my childhood to a tiny, mobile home my wife and I shared with my in-laws, to a series of homes, houses, and apartments of various sizes in various cities. But what this book is mostly about is our sometimes frustrating fifteen-year search for, and two-year renovation of, "the perfect living space" that led finally to a wonderful loft in downtown Toronto. Not, I hasten to add, one of those popular, trendy, developer lofts sprouting up all over the place in condo buildings or refurbished warehouses.

Loft dwellers, it is important to understand, come in two categories: those who buy these airy, open-plan dwellings ready-made or virtually ready-made, and those who, perhaps out of some masochistic urge or untreated childhood neurosis, insist on starting from scratch and getting deeply ensnared in the whole tedious process of finding, buying, designing, gutting, and renovating. We, as you will discover, were in the second category. And this is the inside story of that wearying and convoluted process.

Ten years later and still ecstatic in our awesome dwelling, we are unlikely to undertake an exercise like this again any time soon. Nor, for that matter, am I likely to write another book on this subject. Your careful attention to this one, therefore, would be greatly appreciated, certainly by me and hopefully by you. Here's what you can expect: Part I documents our search; Part II lets you in on the many challenges of doing the renovation; and Part III shares what life is like on the inside. This book will, I hope, appeal to those who

are considering following in our tortuous path (with my ecstatic and/or bombastic utterances either egging them on or scaring them off). And it may also, perhaps, provide vicarious pleasure for the more sensible.

My parents came to Canada as youngsters before the First World War, arriving without a kopeck or a zloty, depending on which side of the disputed, constantly shifting, Russian/Polish border they came from. No one – neither my parents nor their peers – knew for sure.

My mother, just twelve, managed to get four months of public school and learn a little English before having to go to work to help support her impoverished family. Although her academic career was, to her lifelong regret, short-lived, she loved every fleeting moment of it and talked about the joy of her brief educational experience all her life.

Today, the loft that took us fifteen years to find and two years to renovate, in the church that found us, is just across the way from a public school. We can see the school building through our windows and from our front door. By a remarkable coincidence, it's the very same public school my mother attended in 1912.

Every day, as I go out the door and look towards the school, I think of my mother as a little girl, walking to school, playing in the schoolyard, and loving the class she was in. If she were alive today, I'm sure she would have thought we were nuts to be living in a loft. But I know she most certainly would have enjoyed the coincidence of the loft's location.

Here's to you, Ma.

Acknowledgments

I'm grateful to architect and friend, Richard Drdla, not only for the excellent design of our loft renovation itself but also for his wise counsel regarding a number of infelicities in the manuscript, mostly architectural, but sometimes chronological and occasionally attitudinal – now happily corrected or expunged. I owe thanks to John Dalla Costa, who brought scholarly insights and authorial experience to his critique of the manuscript. And also to my daughter, Lori, and my son, Brad, for reading the manuscript and offering sometimes wry, but always helpful, comments.

Needless to say, I'm deeply indebted to my wife and lifelong companion, Colleen, for her unflagging determination to keep the renovation and me on target and also for her invaluable contributions as adviser, proofreader, editor, critic, photographer and hand holder. As partner and resident visionary, she proved far more accurate in her predictions than I – she was almost one hundred percent correct. Without her clairvoyance and her insistence on forging ahead, the project might have come to naught. I wish also to acknowledge the contributions of our friend, digital artist/photographer Linda Corbett of Eyeris Interactive Inc. and also of Colleen Dagnall of Colleen Dagnall Photography, whose excellent recent photography of our lofty enterprise brilliantly supplements Colleen's historical and later photos.

Some of my thinking was inspired by a lovely book, *The Un-Private House,* by Terence Riley, chief curator of the department of architecture and design at New York's Museum of Modern Art. The book accompanied a MOMA show of the same name. I am grateful to both Terence Riley and MOMA. Finally, I want to thank my agent, Matie Molinaro, and her in-house associate, Julius Molinaro, not merely for representing me but also for their encouragement and patient guidance.

CLUMP

Not all stories can begin at the beginning. Some stories have to start in the middle, because sometimes something in the middle of the story stands out in memory for its iconic quality, its air of mystery, its irony, or its prescience. And, of course, when that happens, the middle of the story becomes the beginning, the key to the telling of the tale, the hinge on which the whole tale turns. The middle of this story happened on an autumn day in 1991 when my wife, Colleen, and I and a real estate agent came upon a humdrum clump of buildings on a residential street in the west end of downtown Toronto. Clump may be an odd word to describe buildings, but a clump is what they looked like. Moody and silent, the clump huddled against a dark sky on that rainy afternoon with about as much charm as a mausoleum. We weren't in the market for a mausoleum. We'd been looking for a loft space and weren't having much luck when we'd come by chance upon this clump. Come by chance? It sounds like a port in Newfoundland. That day, it may as well have been Newfoundland. The weather certainly was.

The agent, whose name was Stephen, had been chauffeuring us around Little Italy, which, despite the label, was neither little nor any longer exclusively Italian. It was now very much a multi-ethnic neigh-bourhood and already in the throes of urban renewal. We'd been driving around this area for a couple of hours, when what should loom up on our left but this pile of not particularly prepossessing masonry. Truth to tell, if I'd been the driver, I'd have tromped on the pedal and driven on. But Stephen was behind the wheel. Never one to miss an opportunity to be informative, he stopped the car directly across the street from what we could now see was a church and a church hall. Hmm, I thought. A church? A church might have possibilities. We could build a loft in a church. Our trusty guide, however, proceeded to draw our attention not to the church but to the parish hall immediately next to the hulking house of worship.

Huddled against a dark sky, the church and church hall may, in retrospect, have been a cluster rather than a clump. These things are subjective.

The church hall was, as best we could make out in the rain and rapidly fading light, a rectangular receptacle of no particular distinction; a rather charmless utilitarian structure, even less engaging than the holy edifice that was its companion.

"For your information and possible interest," Stephen said, "the church hall to the left of the church has just been sold to a developer and . . ."

Stephen's earnest discourse was interrupted when suddenly, on our right and out of the red rather than the blue – it was, after all, a fire hall – all hell broke loose. Overhead doors shot up, lights blinked and flashed, sirens screamed and hooted, and three long red engines of succour hurtled out onto the busy street, bringing traffic to a halt and passing within inches of us, to be followed only seconds later by the fire chief in his equally red but somewhat shorter station wagon.

"As I was saying," Stephen said, unfazed, "the church hall is about to be sold to a developer. He plans to add another floor and make it into condominiums."

"Condominiums?" Colleen and I shook our heads and grimaced in unison.

"Oh, these will not be typical condominiums," explained Stephen. "These will be loft condos."

We were dead set against condos of any description, I reminded Stephen, loft or otherwise. Condos were not us. Space was what we were after. Big space. We had pretensions to – or perhaps it was delusions of – bigger, better, grander things. We saw ourselves as space seekers on a quest for the holy grail of downtown loft living, daring adventurers determined to discover a wild, wacky, wonderful edifice – an obscure structure, perhaps hidden away somewhere and hitherto unheralded, an unrecognized gem, rich with infinite possibilities but within our – ahem – finite price range, a place with space and grace that we could miraculously transform into the high, wide, and handsome loft residence of our wildest imaginings.

"Not to worry," Stephen assured us. "I haven't forgotten. I'm merely pointing out options for your information."

I looked again at the cheerless church lurking in the murk, as the fleet of fire engines, now returning from their sortie, beep, beep, beeped their backward way into their narrow, elongated repositories. Back so soon? False alarm, I thought.

"Forget about the church hall, Stephen. What about the church itself? Is the church for sale?"

"Yes, as a matter of fact it is. But it's too big. Even the developer passed on it. It's way too big for just the two of you. It would take several families to handle that much space. To make it work, you'd have to find partners to go in with you or rent out part of it."

Colleen and I had been over that ground thoroughly and had decided early on that we wanted no part of either partners or tenants. As we drove off, I looked back at the church. Damn! Another miss in our long hunt for a loft space. Another false alarm.

CHASING SPACE

Only in middle age did I realize that my fascination, nay, obsession, with living space might have had something to do with the space that my impecunious immigrant family lived in when I was a child. My parents, my sister, and I rented the small, second-floor flat we called home from another immigrant family, a group of six (one more and they might have become famous Canadian painters) who themselves rented the whole three storey house, which they could afford only with the aid of our monthly rent contribution. As tenants of tenants in an immigrant area in downtown Toronto, we were just another tenuous link in the short chain of affordability. The chain was constricting. One bathroom on the second floor, right at our kitchen door, served all ten bodies in the house. And busy bodies they were. The morning rush was madness. Even during slack times, a bath required a booking.

Two adults, two children; we four restless souls squeezed uncomplainingly – indeed, gratefully – into three tiny rooms: kitchen, bedroom, and postage stamp-sized parlour, which, with a pullout studio couch, doubled as a second bedroom. Privacy was a theoretical concept. (We may have been ahead of our time. Today, with bank machines, cell phones, the Internet, and the increasing piracy of personal data, privacy is once again becoming a theoretical concept.) If, in our confined living space, everybody was in everybody else's way (or "face," as we say now), we didn't fuss over it. We took it as normal. Spaciousness was, after all, a luxury

A house today that I lived in during my childhood. We rented the second floor from the renters who rented the first floor and the attic.

affordable only by the rich. We were not among them. We knew our place. And it was small.

So small, in fact, that there was no room in our constricted abode to play indoors. Playing indoors was out; playing outdoors was in. I now realize, post facto, that as kids we survived our cramped quarters by staying out of them as much as possible. Back then we were all street kids. I was a big kid and grew bigger while going to three public schools, where if I set any records, they were not academic but related to my size. Despite always being the youngest in the class I had started school at the age of three I towered over my classmates. In the one high school I attended, helping to pay my way by working at summer jobs from the age of twelve on, I was notable for my round-shouldered slouch, bad posture,

and lack of interest in all things athletic. This, fortunately, did not interfere with my graduating, enabling me to go on to the University of Toronto where, testing the job market at intervals, I dropped in and out and in again over a five-year period, finally wangling a degree. My extensive list of employment postings following my graduation is another book, which I do not intend to write. Suffice to say, I chased after jobs that appealed to me wherever they happened to be. This led me to Western Canada where in Regina, Saskatchewan, over a nine-year period, my occupational activities included sales with a brokerage firm, a real estate company, and a TV station; management of a car wash and a restaurant; and editing and publishing an entertainment magazine. Some of the foregoing were sequential, some not. All ultimately were disappointments if not outright failures. Oh, and did I mention that I did a kid's hand puppet show on TV? The show was dropped when, after a successful run, its ingeniously disguised satire was discovered by management who deemed it too adult for little minds. Management may have had the little minds. Or it may have been me.

In Regina, I met Colleen, a lifeguard at a public swimming pool, and went off the deep end. She was still in college and was also a member of a ballet group. When we married two years later, she was starting to dance professionally and also to teach ballet. So in a nutshell, I grew up, wandered, and wed. And then, Colleen and I continued to wander. Nomads, that's what we were: job changers, home jugglers, space shifters. And after our two kids were born, we became a travelling family troupe that relocated frequently and fearlessly.

As a consequence of our vagabondage, Colleen and I and, at times, our daughter Lori and our son Brad and our various dogs, birds, fish, and turtles (the cockroaches were not ours) had lived in or hoped to live in or contemplated living in or should have lived in many, many different kinds of digs. Any notions I've acquired about living space are undoubtedly a byproduct of all our moving around.

After our marriage, while looking for a place to live in Regina – we hadn't heard of lofts yet – we accepted Colleen's parents' invitation to camp in with them ... but there were a few wrinkles. They were living in a mobile home (a deliverable home really, mobile only during delivery) forty miles away in Moose Jaw. (Moose Jaw, a small Saskatchewan city notable for . . . well . . . for its name, had once been a major railway terminus. After the railway terminated its terminus and dropped dead in its tracks, Moose Jaw, despite being on the prairie, went downhill.)

A triumph in compression, the mobile home was the smallest space we ever inhabited. The bathroom – wash basin, toilet bowl, and shower – fit into an enclosure the size of a phone booth. In addition to self, you showered basin, bowl, and floor and then had to decide what to dry first: skin, porcelain, or floor tiles.

Every morning, we drove – damply – to Regina, seeking a dwelling. Finally, after two months in a not-really-mobile home in Moose Jaw, we moved

Yesteryear. Colleen and I and her mom (in shorts) in front of the narrow mobile home in Moose Jaw. That's her dad behind the camera. We narrowly escaped to Regina.

into a not-really-well-designed home in Regina, a frame bungalow of wood siding, advertised as:

```
spacious, three bedroom bung.
with den, two bathrooms, L-shaped
living/dining room with large
picture windows overlooking
attractive corner lot.
```

Unbeknownst to us, it was a bungled, basementless bungalow designed with only a crawlspace, by its previous owner. After it was built, the demon designer decided it needed a basement. Whereupon, he started to dig one under the finished structure, removing soil in buckets, only to discover mid-dig that for the bungalow not to implode into the intended basement, concrete supporting walls would have to be built inside the original footings. As labour and costs ballooned, the disgruntled design-it-yourselfer settled for half a job. Result: a very low, partial basement which we inherited, when we took the offbeat bungle off the much-wrung hands of its creator.

Despite idiosyncratic underpinnings, this bungalow served us well. Lori and Brad were born while we lived there, and the house worked for them. Still, five years later, when we decided to move up to a new house, there were few (i.e., zero) buyers for our atypical bungalow. Fortunately, the sales manager of the new development proposed that we buy the new dwelling while under construction, and if we hadn't sold our bung by the time the new house was ready, he would take the old one in trade.

And that was how we traded our funny bunny-galow for a splendid, new, award-winning two-storey with high ceilings; floating maple staircase; huge, white block fireplace with a stone bench hearth running the length of the living room; and broadloom extending as far as the eye could see, maybe to the horizon. We never had time to find out. A few months later, accepting a job offer, we left Regina.

Notwithstanding its glories, our prairie palace proved

The basementless bungled bungalow in Regina looked surprisingly good on the surface. But down deep it was shallow.

unsaleable. The location, location, location was right on. But in the depressed prairie real estate market, the timing, timing, timing was right off. And we were afflicted with a six-year plague of tenants, some given to midnight flits, rent unpaid. Still, we managed to keep the not-so-little house on the prairie mostly rented and mostly paid for, while we tried in vain to flog it. The white elephant had become an albatross. And I had become a cheerless student of living spaces, an early step in my career in space.

The next step was Winnipeg where I sold TV time for a year. While a year in Winnipeg is not a year in Provence, it had its moments, but unfortunately, not all that many.

So it was next to a Toronto ad agency. Our Regina house still unsold, we paid the mover by selling most of our possessions. Farewell, Winnipeg! Your winters were cold. Your summers were hot. Your mosquitoes were merciless. But your natives were friendly.

What chattels remained went to Toronto by van, while we went by car. We had arranged to arrive the same day as the van, so we could move directly into the apartment we'd rented on an earlier visit. We arrived as planned. But the van didn't. It disappeared off the map but was finally located with a broken an axle, which took five days to replace, in a northern Ontario town. My advice: never break an axle in Kapuskasing. Unless it's absolutely necessary.

We would have preferred to live downtown in Toronto, but what was available was not affordable. And what was affordable was not available. Fortunately, our earlier visit had produced my new job and an affordable – albeit not downtown – three-bedroom apartment in a low-rent, low-rise in Don Mills, in the northern part of the city. For $135 a month, it was, as they said on ancient Sanskrit stone carvings, a godsend, with an on-site playground and swimming pool and nearby schools. We settled in for two years, our kids, at school, I, at work. We made friends, saved a little money and started thinking about living more graciously. And when we discovered a new, award-winning rental townhouse complex hidden in the trees across the street from us, we moved across the street.

Clustered on the edge of a wooded ravine, the airy, artfully conceived, two-storey townhouses with full, high basements were open plan with half-walls and wide window openings that let in light lending a feeling of spaciousness.

Each house had its own walkout patio surrounded by well-maintained grounds with plenty of recreational areas and a huge swimming pool. Living only feet from the street, yet invisible from it, was like living in the country. It was one of the nicest homes we ever lived in. We were there for three years. (The first time.)

But sitting still was not to last. Ever mobile and seeking personal renewal, we up and moved to Baltimore, Maryland, on two-year student passports to go back to school, I to Johns Hopkins grad school to pursue creative writing and Colleen to Goucher College and Towson State University to study English literature. Retreads, we were called. Our kids, ages twelve and ten and still in grade school, were just regular treads but they insisted on accompanying us. To help finance our reckless academic adventure, we accepted a low offer on our house in Regina, adding insult to penury and settling for twenty-five percent less than our original cost. Finally, after six years of hassles and three home moves, we managed to unload it. Farewell, albatross. Hello, Baltimore.

In Ballimur, as the natives call it, we rented an affordable garden apartment, with the help of a fellow student whose father had been a friend of minimalist architect Ludwig Mies van der Rohe. (Less about Mies later.) On a greenbelt in the core, these apartments were, in effect, one-level, red brick townhouses stacked three high on top of each other. Their special appeal: entering your apartment from your own wood, concrete, and metal porch, reached by outside stairs.

Three bedrooms meant ample space, and end of the row meant windows and light on three sides. Importantly, air-conditioning kept summer (over 100 degrees Fahrenheit) at bay. Two years flew by. Time for us to fly.

We'd arranged to move back into one of the

The Don Mills apartment building in Toronto. Affordability just when we needed it. And we needed it.

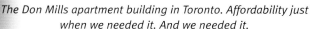
6

The academic retreads in front of the Baltimore garden apartments. No sign of their offspring – the treads. They must have been taking the picture.

ance, and from my mother, who, eager to see us settled, trusted us with her meagre savings. For five years, on grounds that were a gardener's delight, a lawn-cutter's dilemma, and a snow-shoveller's challenge, we lived suburban style, in a

```
3 BR rambling ranch bung., L-shaped LR/DR,
picture windows, high, finished basement,
rec room, double garage, driveway, wide,
deep lot, landscaped lawns front and back.
```

Our domicile was one of ten on a court, an enclave, green, serene, yet somehow too pristine, too nicely manicured; vaguely posh, slightly snotty, anonymous, a still life. No sidewalks, only an occasional car, and no people to be seen – no one on foot, no kids playing, no children's voices in the distance.

People came out their doors and, hidden from the street by hedges, shrubbery, planters, breezeways, carports, garages, attitudes, and indifference, they got into cars and drove off to office or shopping centre. Except for occasional dog walkers like us and the odd, sweaty jogger who wasn't

user-friendly Don Mills townhouses on our return to Toronto. Our unit, right on the edge of the ravine, was even nicer than the first. Again, we lived there for three years. Then, as we got our lives and our finances organized (I was a visiting associate professor teaching creative writing at the University of Toronto, and Colleen was a film editor in TV commercial production) we began thinking again about buying a house downtown. The directors of our children's division, now ages sixteen and fourteen, were not eager to leave their friends and schools. (Lori had been in eight schools in nine years; she'd had enough.) So we agreed to look nearby. We soon found a place we liked but couldn't quite afford. After mulling it over, we opted to go for it anyhow and then scrambled to raise the down payment.

Prospects improved, we borrowed against insur-

The award-winning townhouse development in the trees, on the ravine. Hidden from the street, it was out of sight, man.

about to stop and chat, there was no street life. Still, we had five good years there. Our kids liked it. We enjoyed the space, the grounds, and the feeling of ownership, especially after we were able to pay back borrowed money.

We had fun decorating, installing golden-orange, wall-to-wall carpet that made the sun seem to shine in our living room even at night, and painting the walls a hypnotic dark charcoal gray. While there, the housing market went through the roof. We expected that when we came to sell the house, it would sell quickly. Five years later, we finally put the house on the market. It would be our first profitable real estate transaction ever. It gave us the wherewithal to explore a new lifestyle. With our kids away at school (Lori at Dalhousie University and Brad in residence at the University of Toronto), at last, we could see our way downtown.

THINKING BIG

In thinking about the sort of place we wanted to live in, it became clear that what we wanted was space – space to breathe in, to stretch out in, to flex our muscles in, to flex our minds in, to be creative in. From articles about live/work loft spaces often accompanied by striking photos, the loft word entered our everyday vocabulary.

Once it had imprinted itself in our minds, we couldn't leave it alone. We knew we wanted to live in a loft and embarked on what would become an on-again, off-again search for loft space that eventually led us to . . .

But I'm getting ahead of myself. I should clarify what I mean by loft. I don't mean those popular, newly built, loft

9

One of the boats we missed. This building behind the Art Gallery of Ontario had been built onto and could have been built into a great loft.

eye and warm the heart and can be lived in and lived with. More art than architecture, the end result is not merely more living space but living space enriched by the innovative responses to those happy accidents of structure with which the old building was blessed and which must be dealt with in the conversion.

Where did lofts come from? Historically, a loft was an upper space, sometimes under a sloping roof, in a hall, church or barn, like a choir loft, or a hayloft, or sometimes, the wide-open, upper level of an old industrial building. Later, as indigent artists needed to live and work in large, low-cost space, loft came to mean the upper storey of a warehouse or small factory building, generally a high-ceilinged, big-windowed, open space with good, natural light, no inside walls or partitions, and (often) exposed pillars, beams, boards, pipes, and ductwork.

apartments. ("Soaring 9 foot ceilings," says a recent ad.) They're well designed, maximize small space by leaving it open, let in the light, are fun to live in, and they're good value. But they're open-plan apartments, not true lofts. True lofts weren't originally built to be lived in but for some other purpose. What makes loft creation so intriguing is that it forces the architect/designer to work within parameters initially fixed for an entirely different purpose. And he or she has to do so in a way that not only overcomes the original purpose but also conjures up an end product that is artful, aesthetically pleasing and pragmatic. It is, after all, going to be lived in.

This challenging task takes the designer beyond the world of design into the world of leading edge postmodern art; the world of deconstruction, of new and unlikely juxtapositions, of striking combinations and myriad materials and diverse media that confound old rules yet gladden the

The search for this last kind of loft space took us on a merry chase around the Toronto core for the three months before we had to move from our Don Mills digs. We were in and out of factories, dairies, machine shops, garages, bakeries, warehouses, storefronts, some vacant, some derelict, some in old, polluted areas unfit for habitation. Our search was further complicated by our insistence that we would not renters be. We had to owners be. And, if we were to owners be, we had to buyers be. But what was for sale was massive, expensive, complicated, inaccessible, polluted or, due to zoning laws, illegal. Toronto's archaic zoning restrictions, rigidly administered, forbade living in buildings designated for other purposes. Industrial buildings were not to be lived in, lest they screwed up the tax base, diminished the job base, overloaded the sewers, made increased demands on the power supply, overtaxed the water supply, slowed up garbage removal, contravened

10

the fire safety regulations, and caused cavities.

As industry and commerce were seduced out of the core by suburban tax holidays and low-cost land inducements, downtown buildings increasingly emptied out and were in danger of becoming derelict. It took a few years, but finally someone figured out that a depopulated core would die. Urbanologist Jane Jacobs, who now lives in Toronto, figured out some thirty years before (*The Death and Life of Great American Cities*), that loft living would repopulate the downtown core, keep it alive. Today, with the rules changed, that's what's happening. The core is hot. But when we started our search, it was not.

Still, we kept searching. There wasn't much available but we did see three possibilities which, in hindsight, we should have bought. Behind the Art Gallery, a funny two-storey building, which, having been built onto, rambled all over

Another building we missed out on, now a popular pub. The carwash next door that made me balk is long gone. It was torn down shortly after I balked.

View looking east on the street where the old "bedding plant" was on the left.

the lot. We both reacted positively. Colleen, who has always been an excellent visualizer – she scores in the ninety-ninth percentile in spatial perception tests – could see possibilities right off. Long empty, the building had been waiting for someone with a high spatial perception score. But I saw only a costly renovation and balked. Nearby, in a block of rundown, mostly unused, old factories and warehouses, stood a narrow, deep, three-storey structure that had housed a mattress maker (which made it a bedding plant). It was ideal. But with major roof damage, leakage and parking problems, we backed off. A little west, we saw a big, bright, high-ceilinged, vacant, two-storey building with wonderful windows and a great old wooden floor. It had parking and the price was right. Conversion would have been easy, until I spotted the carwash, which I refused to live next to. All three properties had one thing in common besides my rejection. They were in an area soon to be the hottest redevelopment district in town. Fortunes were paid and made. But not by us.

Having to move soon but making no headway in our search, we looked at some non-loft possibilities. A renovated Victorian on a tree-lined street, midtown, handy to shopping and the subway, caught our fancy:

```
Beautiful, bright, 4 BR, Victorian, architec-
turally renovated, fully upgraded 3-storey,
on  excellent downtown street, open plan LR
and DR, huge master with ensuite, second
floor sitting room, bright sunroom with
skylights, looks out on lovely yard, back
lane parking for 2 cars.
```

The architect owner had gutted the interior, replaced the bearing walls with a beam and pillars and torn out the outside back wall, extending the space into a spectacular sun porch, glassed all around and skylighted above. Sliding glass doors opened onto an attractive backyard. The illusion of spaciousness was remarkable. There'd been no offers. We quickly made an offer under the asking price, and prepared to inch up. It was signed back with an asking price closer to the original. Before we could say yes, came another offer for slightly more than we had decided to agree to. Our agent advised offering the original asking price. But the next day, a third offer for the original asking price preempted both other offers. We won the battle by paying more than the asking price. We never regretted it. We stayed in the old Vic fourteen years, an all-time record for us.

Midtown beat the "burbs" by a city mile. But ultimately, we started thinking lofts again. Maybe, it was time to move. We put the Victorian on the market. And the first looker made an offer slightly less than the asking price. The delighted agent urged us to accept. But with no pressure to sell, we signed the offer back for the full asking price. The buyer agreed. The house was his, possession in six months.

Time to get our act together. We were moving again.

The front entrance to the Victorian.

CHAPTER 4

SEARCH AND RESEARCH

Proceeds of house sale in hand, we began searching for loft space without result. Then, one night in a movie lineup, we got talking to Richard Drdla, an architect and urban planning consultant. Omaha born, he had graduated in architecture from MIT, worked in London for seven years on the Milton Keynes new towns development and then in Toronto for a New York architectural firm. With non-conventional housing and livable cities among his chief areas of expertise, he had, for the last few years, been a consultant, mostly on affordable housing policy. To maintain his design skills, he liked from time to time to undertake small design projects. Lofts were small design projects. We had lucked into an expert who understood precisely our lofty intentions and was also familiar with the city core. Richard offered to help in our search, unpaid, until actual design work started. He could help make it happen. We couldn't believe our good luck. Thus began a long-term friendship.

We often prowled back lanes with Richard, checking out loft possibilities. Sometimes, we went looking with real estate agents. Not much was available. Besides, most agents would have preferred to show us conventional residential properties. That's what they knew. That's what was in their computers, files, books, systems, minds, and hearts. Many puzzled over our persistent quest for a loft. Why would you want to live in a loft when you could have a traditional home, tried and true, in a good residential area, or a nifty penthouse in the sky from which on a clear day you can see Niagara Falls? (Or Buffalo. Or smog. Or the traffic jams on the Gardiner Expressway. Or the accounting department of the Toronto-Dominion Bank.) For most real estate people,

lofts existed only in movies and magazines. Mostly, in Toronto anyway, they were right.

On one of our searches, we met Harry, a real estate agent whose success selling condos crowned him Condo King. (He was the first. There has been a series of pretenders to the throne ever since.) When he couldn't find us a building to renovate, we put a deposit on a townhouse in a condo development that Harry was planning to build downtown. Because land assembly was not completed, our deposit was held in trust and refundable. But, with the development schedule unfinalized, pinning down a possession date was impossible.

"We've sold our house and have to be out soon," I reminded Harry.

"Don't worry," said Harry. "I'll find you a condo to rent for a year. By then, your townhouse will be ready."

And he did. And we did. But it wasn't. In fact, it never happened at all. But we didn't find that out till later.

In the meantime, to tide us over, Harry found us a condo rental in a ten-storey tower in the old Town of York. An appealing area, and as downtown as you could get, just a block from the bustling St. Lawrence Market, a lovely place to be, surrounded by interesting restored buildings, old churches, little hidden green spaces, courtyards, and open squares. Standing on the street and looking west, you were awestruck by the skyline of imposing towers that seemed to hang in the near distance, glinting and shimmering in the sunlight by day, twinkling in the darkness by night. Not a day went by that we didn't comment on the grandeur of the view. And the rent was pretty grand, too, sixteen times what we paid to rent our first apartment in Toronto. Still, since

The rental condo building. With all that glass, you'd expect it to be light on the inside. But only the corner units had decent light.

the condo was leased only for a year and we were solvent from our house sale, we didn't complain. But sixteen times the rent!

Pets had once been welcome in the building. But the pet policy had just been changed. Pets already in residence could stay. But pet newcomers were unwelcome. We were between dogs at the time, but condo management granted visiting privileges to our son Brad's two wheaten terriers, who came to visit. Two days before moving into our new premises, unexpectedly, we acquired one of the wheatens – the four-year-old male, Satch – not for a visit, but to stay, to be ours. My son and his wife had bought Satch as a puppy. When he was about two years old, they decided he needed company and got another wheaten puppy, Zoë, a female. The two dogs got along well, and everybody was happy. Then, Brad and Jane had their first child, a son, and less than two years later, they had a second son. This combination didn't work, and, well . . .

We've had Satch for ten years as I write this, and he's never given us any trouble. After two days with us, Satch moved into the condo as a "visitor" and never left. With 2,400 square feet of condo, he had space to roam – a vast living room, a giant dining room, two huge bedrooms, two bathrooms (one ensuite in the master bedroom), as well as a powder room at our front door, plus a storage and utility room the size of a guest room, or airplane hangar.

The light in the condo, however, was a disaster. Thanks to the thirty feet wide by eighty feet deep design, all the windows were on one of the thirty-foot ends in a pseudo-solarium. The only natural light was at the window end; the rest of the eighty-foot length was dark all day. The kitchen on the farthest wall from the windows, and almost eighty feet from outside light, was midnight around the clock. So was the dining room and it didn't help when we turned on the ghastly chandelier. The living room, wired to be lit by eight floor lamps and we had only two, was equally dim. We quickly learned that the first task every morning was to turn on every light in the place. This increased our electricity bill without solving our lighting problem. After Colleen talked me out of

The view looking west outside our rental condo was breathtaking. Mind you, with your head back and your mouth open, people regarded you suspiciously.

T h e   U r b a n   L o f t

*The gargoyle with his water cut off for the cold winter weather.
No one likes a gargoyle with icicles.*

tain, a stone gargoyle watered a stone basin. Once in a while, a passing drunk attempted to join the gargoyle and had to be shooed off by the bright, affable, helpful, around-the-clock concierges who manned the front desk. Jocular small talk invariably preceded the pushing of the button that electrically unlocked the door from the vestibule into the purposeless, always empty, unnecessarily large lobby. After a while, it occurred to me that the electrically controlled entrance made us, in effect, a gated community, which is too fortress-like for my taste, and not my idea of a community.

After a few months, we learned that Harry's condo development might not happen. The developers were beset with problems. Hoping that increased funding would keep the loft venture aloft until the problems could be solved, the developers raised the price of the condos and asked the purchasers-in-waiting to increase their deposits. We realized then that the project was beyond us financially and regretfully withdrew. Our deposit was refunded immediately.

If Harry had any other loft possibilities for us, we never heard, since he was, unfortunately, too busy scrambling to deal with his own project as it slowly unravelled and then, sadly, fell apart. A dream concept, gone. Another loss for the visionaries.

smashing the chandelier, we made the pseudo-solarium into our dining room so we could eat by the windows in natural light. This meant transporting food and dishes back and forth the eighty-foot length of the apartment. It felt like take-out.

Despite the design deficiency that made our apartment the heart of darkness, there were some positive things about the building. The en-trance was nice: unimposing, unostentatious – flutes rather than trumpets. Under a stone archway, almost unnoticeable from the street, a little cobbled roundabout led to the front door. In a small central foun-

CHAPTER 5

A CHURCH?

Then, out of the blue, we got a phone call from a real estate agent named Ric. We'd been out with him looking for loft spaces years before and had forgotten him. Had we ever found our loft? Ric wanted to know. How would we feel about a church? A church? Another church? Good God! Well, what the heck. Why not? A colleague of Ric's had clients about to buy a church, but they had concluded that they couldn't handle the whole holy of holies wholly on their own and were hoping to find someone else to take part of it (thereby turning the holy into a partly). We found the prospect interesting and agreed to have a look.

That's how we found ourselves looking at a Slovakian Roman Catholic church in Toronto's downtown core. When we went to inspect the church, we were transfixed by the shock of recognition. The yellow brick structure in the bright sunlight took us back to a dismal rainy autumn afternoon two years earlier and a dark clump of church buildings lurking in the murk across from a fire hall in front of which we had stopped and looked briefly before driving off.

Omigod! It dawned on us that the Slovakian Roman Catholic church across from the fire hall was, in fact, the very same church we'd stopped in front of with Stephen. More miraculously, this unlikely building on a tranquil (apart from the occasional fire truck) residential street corner in a downtown neighbourhood seemed to fit in well with our lofty intentions. And – yet another miracle – it looked like we could afford part of it.

We took Richard Drdla, who, despite all our peregrinations, was still as loyal to the concept as we were, for a look at the church. He went through the ritual of inspection and then, though without the sprinkling of holy water, he gave it his blessing.

Our search was over. The real fun was about to begin.

Historical photo of church and church hall.
White door on the right is the rectory.

THE CHURCH OF TWO BROTHERS AND OTHERS

A mere make-over, we thought, and spaciousness, graciousness, and good light would soon be ours. A mere make-over? Little did we know how elephantine the task would become as we, the unconverted, converted a church.

Built in 1941, the sturdy, stolid Church of St. Cyril & Methodius had been the spiritual and social centre – and the credit union – of the immigrant Slovakian community then living in the area. It had served them well but unostentatiously. Long and narrow and boxlike, an uninspired and uninspiring edifice of faded yellow brick, it sat stolidly on the street corner rather than rising up triumphantly towards the heavens. Still, on a sunny day, it did not seem like a clump and did not at all resemble the mausoleum with which I compared it the first time I saw it.

Seen from the front, the church was functional rather than eye-catching. The modest front entrance was too close to the sidewalk and only a couple of steps above street level. There was none of the grandeur that one finds, say, in the awesome cathedrals of Europe. Or even in the less awesome cathedrals of Toronto. This was a pragmatic piece of prayer property; a practical, serviceable, workmanlike structure, built not to take the breath away but to provide usable space for its parishioners.

Lord knows, an imposing window treatment would have helped. But the only window with any buzz was the rectangular window over the front door. The largest expanse of glass in the church, it was the most attention-getting pane in an otherwise indifferently glazed structure. The other windows were narrow, slot-like, and, despite the stained glass in them, unremarkable. None of these factors mattered to us. As far as we were concerned, we were buying a space, not a

The churchyard as we found it. And as they left it.
No complaint intended. It was a pretty nice yard.
We just improved it a bit.

The Urban Loft

church. Still, I couldn't help but be intrigued by the fact that the space was a church.

A disclaimer may be in order. I've never been a connoisseur of religious history. Or any history, for that matter. Having said that (and despite tending to the hysterical rather than the historical), I found myself fascinated by the history of the two saints for whom the church was named.

Let's go briefly to Constantinople (now Istanbul), where the not yet saints came marching in. Cyril and Methodius were Greek missionaries after whom a number of churches worldwide were later named, including one in Toronto, half of which was to become ours. I think the fifty percent of the church we got was the Methodius half. But I'm not one hundred percent certain.

As well as being brothers in the church, Cyril (826–869 A.D.) and Methodius (815–884 A.D.) were real-life brothers who became known as the Apostles to the Slavs. Cyril, a church librarian in Constantinople, forsook the books and took to the road on missionary trips with his older brother, Methodius, the abbot of a Greek monastery. Together, the brothers brought the holy word to the Bulgarians and to the Khazars. Interestingly, the Khazars, an ancient, partly nomadic Turkic people who had settled in South Russia between the Volga and the Don, had, about a hundred years earlier (c. 740 A.D.), embraced Judaism. Today, they're believed by some scholars to have been the ancestors of many Russian Jews.

In 862 the brothers were sent by Emperor Michael III to Moravia, which in more recent times (1918) became part of Czechoslovakia. In Moravia, the duo taught and celebrated the liturgy, not in Latin but in the spoken language of the area, the Slavonic vernacular, a previously unwritten tongue, today known – perhaps not to most of us but certainly to theological scholars – as Old Church Slavonic.

The writing was on the wall of the church hall back then, carved in stone. It's gone now, proving not everything carved in stone lasts.

To translate the Bible into this tongue, the brothers, who were also linguists – talk about good planning, or maybe it was heavenly intervention – invented an alphabet based on Greek characters. (Usually, when I think of Greek characters, I think of Zorba. But never mind.) Incidentally, the Cyrillic alphabet of modern Slavic languages, although it gets attributed to St. Cyril, probably came later, the work of his followers. But back to our story.

Determined to enforce the use of the Latin liturgy among the Slavs, the stern German church leadership in Moravia took exception to linguistic unorthodoxy of any kind. The brothers were hauled up on the carpet and had to go to Rome where they were able to successfully defend themselves – or so they thought at the time – against the German accusations.

Cyril died at the age of forty-three in Rome in 869. The more fortunate and longer-lived Methodius was consecrated an archbishop and went back to Moravia as a papal legate. But in 870, the relentless German church authorities, still on his case, put him in prison. Pope John VIII intervened – slowly – and in 873 he was able to get his papal legate released. When, in 884, Methodius died at the age of

The church looking a little less clumpish on a bright sunny day. Isn't sunlight a brilliant concept?

sixty-nine, the missionary brothers became history, later becoming saints and, as noted earlier, lending their names to more than a few churches.

In the course of half a century, the congregation of Toronto's own St. Cyril and Methodius church had slowly moved west and north out of downtown Toronto, to Mississauga. Out where the car is king, the distant edge city of Mississauga has been a runaway success with seekers of bigger lots, lower taxes, and longer commutes. In Mississauga no one walks except to the car or the riding lawnmower. Fortunately, due to the width of the lots, walks to the car or the mower can provide minor aerobic benefits.

Thus it was that the Roman Catholic Archdiocese of Toronto found itself with a surplus church on its hands. In 1991, the church was put on the block, along with the attached rectory and the parish hall next door.

The offering caught the attention of a loft developer who, as we had learned from Stephen, planned to convert the church hall into loft condos. The developer had offered to purchase the church hall himself and help sell the church and rectory to others. The rectory had been snapped up by a couple of smart shoppers – Neil, a chartered accountant, and Sharon, a property manager – who have since restored it, largely with their own four hands (two each), to its quondam glory.

The sale of the former house of worship was more complicated. Though it caught the fancy of a young husband and wife – Michael, a psychiatrist, and Niamh, an art history professor – daring space pioneers both, and veterans (i.e., survivors) of previous space conversions, who envisioned a large-scale, single-family renovation, the church (as Stephen had forewarned) turned out to be too large for one family. Still committed to the concept, however, the determined pair sought partners and were fortunate to find another delusional couple with a similar interest – namely the two of us – to join them in acquiring the once holy but now wholly deconsecrated edifice.

We should have, I suppose, carefully weighed the pros and cons of buying part of a church. After all, the conversion of alternate properties always involves risks, and we'd certainly been risk-averse in the past. But having found what we liked, we just jumped in and made an offer to buy half the church. It was roughly based on market values in the area and all we had to go on. We had never bought half a church before.

Our offer was accepted. With Michael and Niamh, we bought, severed, and divided the church.

The dreaded hassles of renovation began almost immediately. In fact, they began even before the renovation itself began. One of the most puzzling was the hassle over the survey. A survey, of course, was required for the purchase.

The not insubstantial fee paid to the surveyor to provide the survey was shared by the two purchasing couples. A short time later, a second, and identical, survey was required, for reasons none of us understood and still don't understand. It seemed to entail nothing more than having the surveyor provide a copy of the previous survey. Nonetheless, following this, a second bill, equal to the first bill, was sent by the surveyor to the developer of the church hall condo next door, who passed it on to the joint purchasers of the church as our responsibility.

Both our lawyers said we had already paid for a survey and advised us not to pay again. They similarly advised the surveyor. Yet for more than a year, the surveyor dunned all the three parties, developer included, threatening court action while interest mounted up. Finally, the surveyor went to small claims court against the owners of the church. In small claims court the matter was finally settled – and not in our favour. It appeared that legally we owed the surveyor his money. The best that one of our lawyers, who had gone to court on behalf of both couples, was able to do was negotiate the dropping of the interest charges. He threw up his hands (we threw up our lunch) and advised us to bite our tongues and pay the bill.

In any event, as initiators of the project, Michael and Niamh became the proud owners of the front half of the church on the east side of the dividing point, with its dignified front entrance and the choir loft. We became owners of the back half of the church, on the west side of the divide, with its inconspicuous, unassuming – but somehow appealing – side entrance and the altar.

We had half a church to renovate, and a whole architect, whose thinking we liked, to design the renovation and do the drawings. The next thing we needed was a contractor to manage the process. We'd had one in mind for some time. But as it turned out, he had other plans. I had another thought: Why couldn't our architect double as our contractor? I tried this out on Richard. He wasn't sure it was a good idea. The two functions worked best, he felt, when separated. Besides, he was uncertain whether he'd be happy performing the dual function. But I had so much faith in Richard's capabilities that I persisted, using my lately acquired interest in history to make my case. Early architects, I pointed out, called themselves master builders and did it all, design, drawings, construction. Besides, the lost contractor had offered, as a friend, to be available for advice, consultation, recommendations for sub-trades, and so on. I kept after Richard. The matter was finally resolved when Richard agreed that in addition to performing his creative function as architect, he would also – not as contractor, but on our behalf, for a fee – handle the trades.

We didn't realize it at the time, but by making this arrangement with Richard we became, in effect, our own contractors. Let it be known here that we had no hands-on experience in anything to do with construction. We had never built or renovated anything. The hammer and saw were foreign to us. The only things we've ever put together were words. We knew zip about contracting. I can see, in retrospect, how our inexperience as contractors may have contributed to many of the problems I rant about below and try to blame on others.

CHAPTER 7

THE WORK BEGINS

Faced finally with the complexity of the work that lay ahead of us, we were forced to do something about how little we knew. We got busy educating ourselves, collecting tear sheets from magazines and clippings from newspapers of articles on design and photos of converted buildings that appealed to us, of lofts, of layouts of windows, of stairs, of kitchens. The huge file of helpful information that we compiled enabled us, in our regular Sunday-afternoon meetings with Richard, which he insisted be interactive, to make a useful contribution of suggestions and ideas, and not just of unfounded opinions, although we had lots of those, too.

Our architect was not only very creative; he was also very thorough. No detail escaped him. Everything had to be talked through, discussed fully. The meetings were hard work for all of us. And, of course, from the moment the half-church became all ours, the indefatigable Richard had been working night and day on our loft design and on the plans, while at the same time, interviewing, getting bids, hiring subcontractors, and setting up a work schedule.

Best of all, we liked Richard's plans. His design was open and clean and minimalist. On the first floor, for instance, the space would be interrupted as little as possible. Interior walls, where unavoidable, would be partial, or perforated with cutouts, look-throughs, pass-throughs, or glass-block windows. What we were looking for was as much transparency as possible. There would be no doorways and no doors, except on the powder room. (After all, one would not wish to be seen taking a powder.)

The design, like the space in which it was to be executed, was high, wide, and handsome. The living room would be open to the original plaster-on-lath church ceiling that we liked. The height from the living room floor to the highest part of the ceiling was twenty-four feet, the equivalent of two and a half storeys; lofty by any measure. It had been built, as a sort of stepped ziggurat to give the feeling of an arch without actually building an arch, which I'm guessing may have been too costly. After we took down the old overhead fans and light fixtures, the ceiling would need some of the plaster repaired, but that

The interior of the church shortly after the departure of the congregation. Holiness has given way to emptiness and awesome space.

would be much cheaper than putting in a new ceiling. With the living room as the principal space, and therefore the key to the conversion, everything else on the main floor – the entrance hall, dining room, kitchen, powder room and TV room/library – would be tucked under an L-shaped mezzanine.

Our heads were filled with dreams for our loft, but, as we discovered, not all were attainable. When we were converting the space in the church, we occasionally got caught up in a grandiose notion that had to be beaten out of us. Verbally, of course.

Take the stairs, for example. It may have had something to do with the grand staircases we'd seen in architectural magazines; but whatever the reason, our ideas about the stairs in our mecca of minimalism had always been a bit overblown. We wanted a grand staircase, iconic, sculptural, monumental, engineered in steel and glass and wire cable. The climbing colossus would have risen roofward smack in the middle of our spacious premises if we'd had our way.

We didn't. Fortunately, Richard was able to talk us out of this foolishness with a few quick sketches, which made it clear how over-emphasizing the stairs would disrupt the surrounding space, destroying its openness with pretentiousness. He had come up with a simpler idea. The staircase would still be open and visible from almost every area of the house, but it would be stacked to one side on the wall we shared with the rectory. There, it would still feature strongly in the design of the loft but without being overbearing and overwhelming the rest of the space. And it would lead gracefully up to the mezzanine (and eventually, up to the top floor).

The mezzanine would house the master – and only – bedroom, a walk-through dressing room, a bathroom, a laundry room, and an office for me. The bedroom, my office, and the upper hallway would overlook the living room. But unlike the old vaudeville joke, they would not overlook it completely. It was, after all, too big to overlook.

Richard's plan for the basement would contain a two-car garage. The two homes in the church had negotiated an easement with the condo development in the parish hall next door that would let us enter our side-by-side underground garages through the large underground garage just six feet away. The condo garage could be conveniently entered from the wide, well lit, back lane (actually a street, named for yet another saint, Matthias, on whom I've done no research) via a remote-controlled electronic garage door. This would lead down to internal, side-by-side remote-controlled garage doors, which would provide access to the church's two garages.

The basement would also house a utility-cum-storage room. This utility room would stand on the undisguised, beaten-up floor of what was once the stage of the church's basement

Rubble with cause. Renovation requires gutting and gutting means rubble. But rubble doesn't mean anything so it's carted away to the dump.

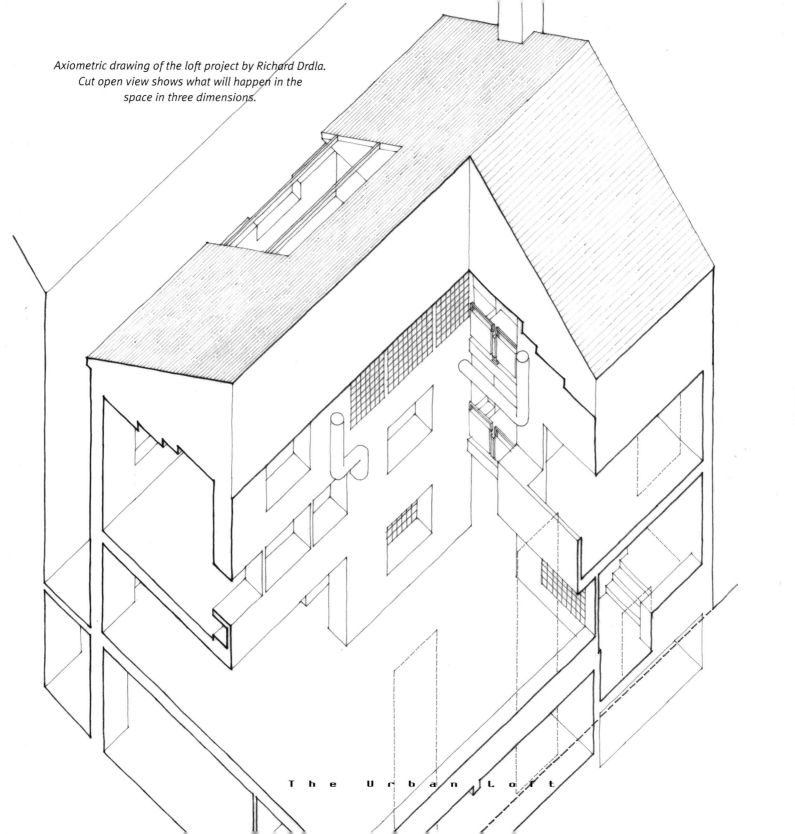

Axiometric drawing of the loft project by Richard Drdla.
Cut open view shows what will happen in the
space in three dimensions.

auditorium. The auditorium itself would become the garage, with the floor being raised four feet to be made level with the floor of the big garage in the church hall next door. This would be accomplished by filling it with our construction rubble and pouring a new concrete floor on top of it.

A studio for Colleen to paint in would be roughed in on the north wall of the basement, which had big windows looking out on the street. Because the windows were so high above ground, the studio floor would be raised a foot and a half with a rough plywood overfloor to bring artist and art closer to the natural light. A nose-in from the garage would be built into the wall between the garage and the studio to allow for the length of the cars. The nose-in, which extended through the garage wall into the studio, would become a counter running the full length of the studio.

We had a lot to do. It was time to get busy.

Like all construction, renovating a loft space requires a building permit. The permit must be applied for. Plans must be submitted and vetted. A substantial fee must be paid. And even then, the permit may be questioned, delayed, or refused for lack of compliance, non-conformity, or other irregularities. Permits take patience.

Since conversions of buildings from non-residential to residential use are almost always non-conforming, building permits can predictably be held up by municipal authorities waiting for the blessings of committees such as the Committee of Adjustment, which generally gives the nod to "minor variances" but often subjects major variances to close scrutiny and sometimes turns them down. This process requires meetings, and meetings take time. The delay inherent in the permit process taxes the patience of most renovators. It taxed mine.

Some of the delay connected with getting the permit, for example, resulted from the fact that the building code demanded on-site parking. Organizing the above-mentioned parking solution, even with the agreement of all parties, involved meetings and discussions and document preparation, all of which took time, precious time, and slowed the process to a crawl. Until the elusive easement was a done deal, the city wouldn't grant the permit.

To be fair, I'll try to keep the moaning down to a murmur and won't recount too many maddening things that happened in the quest for a building permit. Instead, I'll talk only about those that were amusing or instructive. What am I saying? Now I'm in trouble. Everything that happened was either amusing or instructive. (Or expensive. Let's not forget that one.)

Here's an example. After several months of pushing paper at people in power, we – like all renovators do – thought we had all the necessary approvals and expected the permit momentarily so that we could get started on the renovation. We had dates set up with the tradespeople to begin work. Weeks went by. Still no permit. We were having a fit. Our tradespeople couldn't sit around. They had to make a living. We could only stall for so long before losing them to other projects. When – like all renovators do – we started pressing the city for action, we got

The endless debris, there's nothing like it. Except maybe the endless dust, which is even more like it, although few like it.

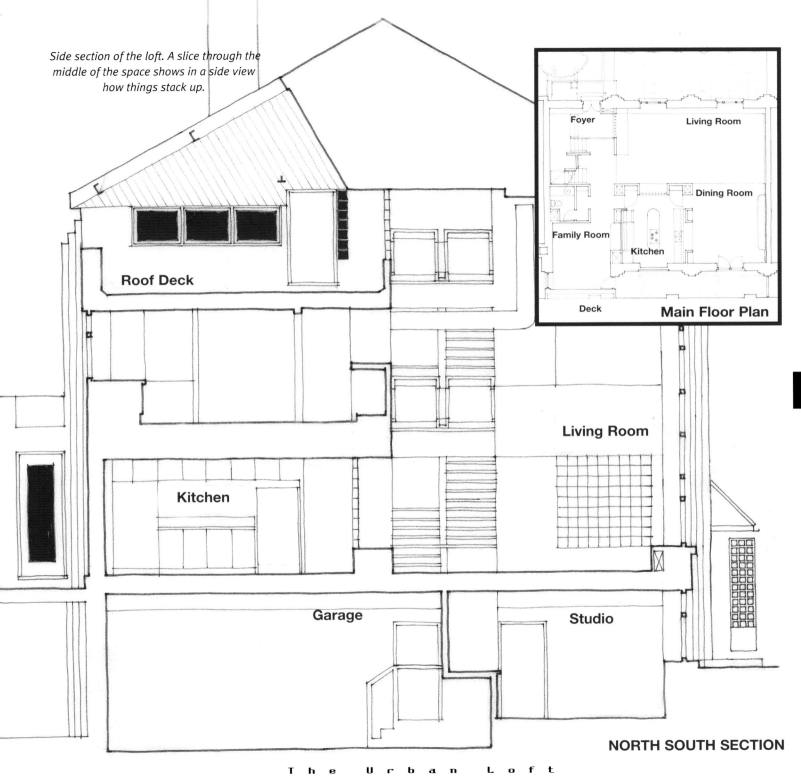

Side section of the loft. A slice through the middle of the space shows in a side view how things stack up.

Roof Deck

Foyer

Living Room

Dining Room

Family Room

Kitchen

Deck

Main Floor Plan

27

Living Room

Kitchen

Garage

Studio

NORTH SOUTH SECTION

The Urban Loft

a series of delayed responses, each of which held us up another week or two. And the delays were not simultaneous. They were sequential.

One response said a document had to go back for the approval of a committee that had been missed. Next sitting in two weeks. Another said the person whose signature was required was out of town for a funeral. He'd be gone for a week. Another said a senior official was on holidays for two weeks. And so on. And slow on.

Before we knew it, we were several weeks behind schedule. Anxious to get going, we rationalized (i.e., schemed) that perhaps if we weren't actually building but were only preparing to build by cleaning up inside of the structure, we could start before we actually got the building permit.

This was not without precedent, we righteously assured ourselves. When the congregation moved out of the church, they had dismantled and removed truckloads of stuff: some of the stained glass windows, most of the pews. They had detached various other attached fixtures, icons, and artifacts – both religious and architectural – to which they were themselves attached, and which they hoped to re-attach in their newly built church. This appeared to have been done without a building permit. Why would they need one? After all, they weren't building, were they?

Well, we thought, that's our rationale. We'll just carry on the pre-building process and clear out the stuff left behind and lying about in our half of the church. Then we'd be ready for the actual construction to start by the time we had the building permit in hand. We were going with our gut.

A gut is a messy business. Gutting the church, with our permit stuck somewhere in administrative limbo, turned out to be doubly so. The politically delicate but physically indelicate – not to mention abysmally dusty – job of gutting our half of the church was given over to a demolition company of Richard's experience, run by a demonic demolisher named Dave, who, because of his bustling "let's-bash-out-that-sucker" style was known to all as Demolition Dave.

Wreckers and razers are not like other tradespeople. Demolishers are, in my view at least, more of a tribe than a trade, with their own dress code, grubby everything, and their own skin colour, gray, probably because they're constantly covered in dust and grime that invades the pores. Which may explain why they arrive at the start of a job first thing in the morning looking as if they've just finished work.

Of course, without a permit, our demolition consultants weren't going to demolish. Oh, no. Absolutely not. They were just going to do a little housekeeping, tidy up a bit. There wasn't even going to be a waste bin, for goodness'

The rubble rises exponentially as the author in the background, oblivious to the wreckage, admires the high, wide, open space and tries not to break into song.

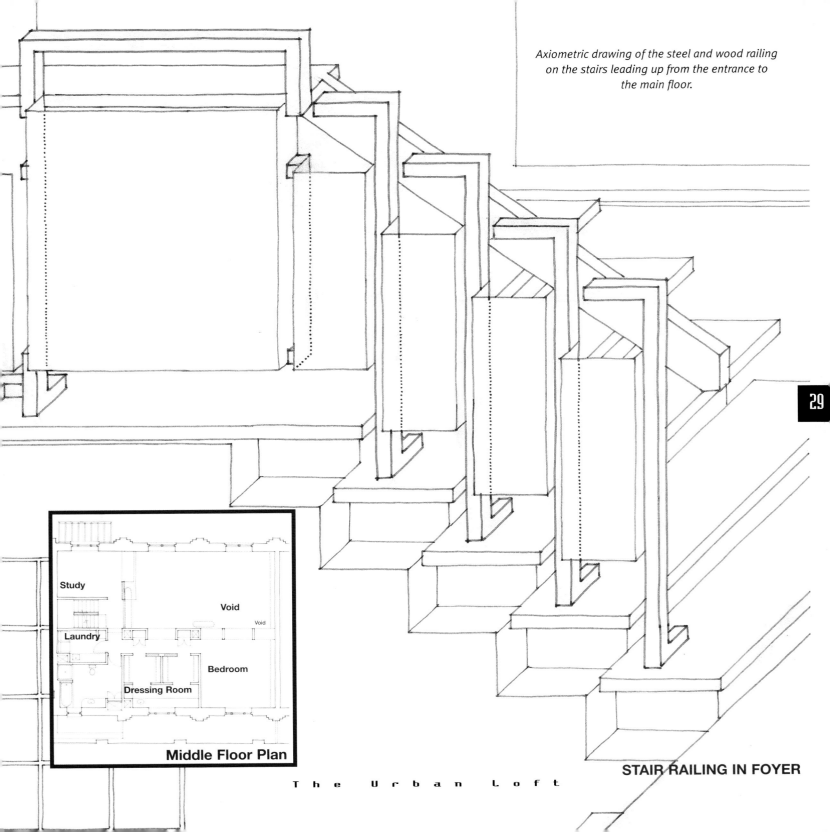

*Axiometric drawing of the steel and wood railing
on the stairs leading up from the entrance to
the main floor.*

Middle Floor Plan

Study

Void

Void

Laundry

Bedroom

Dressing Room

T h e   U r b a n   L o f t

STAIR RAILING IN FOYER

sake. Anything removed would be carted off by truck every so often. We'd rent some scaffolding, of course, because some of the things that had to be taken away were high up on walls.

Still, we hesitated, held off, waiting impatiently, hoping the permit would appear. But it didn't. Finally, we could wait no longer. And so, minus a permit, the – ahem – housekeeping began.

The leftover debris went. Odd bits of broken furniture went. A stained wash basin and a cracked toilet bowl, both unattached and sitting in mid-floor, went. Glass and window frames went. Hanging wires that went nowhere went. Dangly bits of broken piping came down and went. Wall mosaics went. Travertine marble on the walls, breaking as it came off, unfortunately, went. The altar went. Hanging ceiling lights came down and went – but to the basement. We thought we might use them elsewhere later. And later, we did.

Then, one unhappy day, in the midst of all this grime and punishment, the dreaded building inspector came stomping in on the filthy festivities and tore a strip off us for working without a permit. But, sir, we protested, we weren't working "without" a permit, but "prior" to a permit. Despite the clear logic of this explanation, he didn't buy it. We tried "permit pending," but that didn't work either. We explained that we had all the approvals and had been told verbally that the permit had been granted, and we were simply waiting on a little piece of paper that had been stalled by unfortunate administrative circumstances not of our making and having nothing whatsoever to do with the rightness or wrongness of the project itself.

We hoped the inspector would understand our plight and turn a blind eye to our misdemeanours. Instead, he turned a deaf ear to our pleading. Probably due to the fact that most building inspectors have a background in construction, reasoning with one is like talking to a brick wall. This particular brick wall shut us down and sent all the demolishers home. He told us, none too politely, to get out of the building and do no further work of any kind until we had the actual building permit in our hands. I may have imagined it – and Richard is dubious, insisting that city officials are without emotion – but the inspector seemed somehow annoyed, as if we'd betrayed him, as if he was personally aggrieved by our premature activities, as if his feelings had been hurt. And they may have been. I know ours were.

For a week we waited, did nothing. Still no permit. Our phone calls were all in vain. You're in the pile, we were told. We'll get to you. The machine-like apparatus in which we were entangled was incapable of doing anything but going from A to B to C at its own glacial pace.

In desperation, we did what we weren't supposed to do; we went back into the church and started working again. It was either that or have our workmen abandon us for other jobs. Without the people to do the work, you know what we could do with our permit when we got it. Right.

Behind closed doors and with much mess, the church was gutted. The inspectors did not return.

Holy floor, Batman! The havoc as seen looking up from the basement through the hole in the floor under the altar after it was removed.

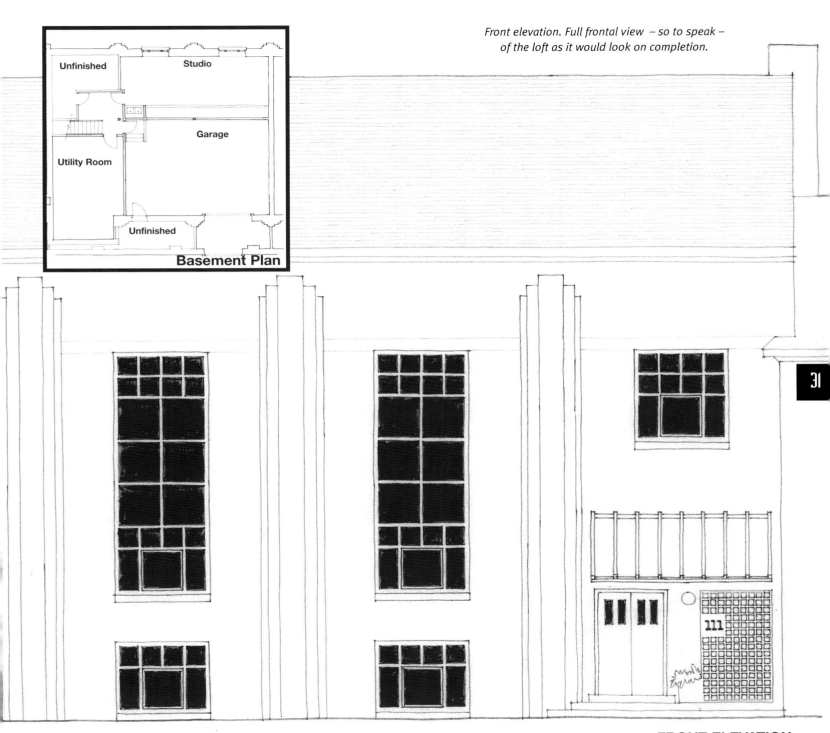

Front elevation. Full frontal view – so to speak – of the loft as it would look on completion.

Basement Plan

Unfinished

Studio

Garage

Utility Room

Unfinished

111

FRONT ELEVATION

The Urban Loft

Sometimes, gut is good.

After the gutting there was something awesome about the emptiness of the building. This take-your-breath-away quality was not simply related to the fact that the structure had been a religious edifice. It was a dimensional rather than spiritual phenomenon. I'd explain it as the volumetric effect of looking from the inside at what, with a little help from our dusty friends, had become a big, empty box. This box, before we cut it into two parts, was ninety feet long, thirty-seven-and-a-half feet wide, and twenty-four feet high, which computes to 81,000 cubic feet. That's a huge heap of cubes. And that didn't include the basement or the space above the ceiling and under the roof.

The main floor was all high, wide, open space. No inside walls. No pillars. Built with I-beams under the floor spanning the entire width of the building, it didn't need supporting walls or pillars. This gave us on the main floor a wide-open platform that could handle almost anything and provided us with the ultimate in flexibility for our own self-centred architectural purposes.

But the main floor was only part of it. Even in the basement with its unexpected fourteen-foot ceiling, there were only two supporting posts. And

above the original – and retained – ceiling of the church, the enormous attic rose a further twelve feet to steel trusses at roof level.

This was the big box, the vast vessel that we would be working in and with. But this awesome openness, this uninterrupted vastness, was about to be interrupted by a demising wall that would cut the space in half and into two lesser but still formidable empty boxes, one of which was ours.

Once you've got an empty box, what you put into it is determined to a great degree by your notions, both philosophical and aesthetic, of how much you want to fill up that emptiness.

How much did we want to fill up our emptiness? Not much. We wanted our loft to be very empty and open – spare, sparse, lean, minimal. Which brings us to minimalism.

Minimalism. What exactly does the term mean? Among certain modernist art, architecture, and design professionals, there's a strongly held attitude that posits that less is more desirable than more. (And conversely, that more is less desirable than less.) This notion – concept, philosophy – is called minimalism; its proponents and practitioners and their hangers-on (among the latter, I include spouse and self) are usually called minimalists. (They've been called other things, as well. But let's not get into that.)

Minimalism originated with one of the leaders of modern functional architecture, Walter Gropius (1883–1969), founder and director, from 1919 to 1928, of Germany's famed Bauhaus school, from which there emanated ideas on architecture that were and still are acclaimed worldwide.

Also linked with the Bauhaus and the functionalist aesthetic of twentieth-century design, Ludwig Mies van der Rohe (1886–1969), another of the pillars of modern architecture, captured the magic of minimalism in a maxim now known around the world. "Less is more," said Mies.

Architect Richard Drdla standing in – or on – the framing and surveying the results of his design. He's smiling, a good sign.

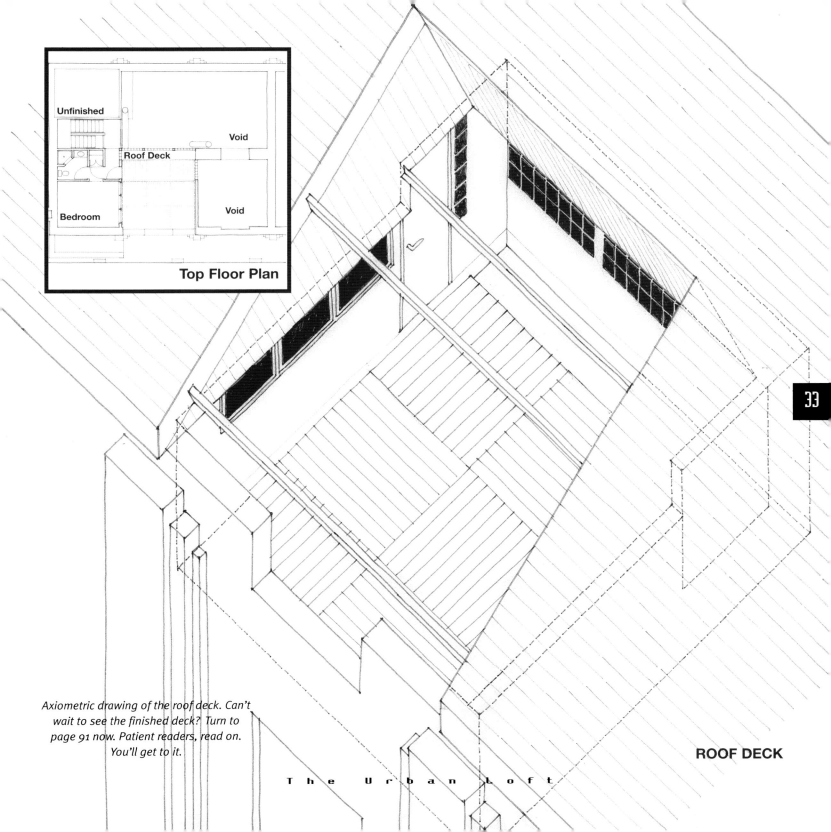

Top Floor Plan

Unfinished

Void

Roof Deck

Bedroom

Void

Axiometric drawing of the roof deck. Can't wait to see the finished deck? Turn to page 91 now. Patient readers, read on. You'll get to it.

ROOF DECK

The Urban Loft

Not everyone, of course, agrees with the maxim or with minimalist thinking. For the purposes of this discussion, and in an attempt at clarification, let's call those who disagree with minimalists, maximalists. And let's call their point of view, maximalism.

That maximalism is the point of view of the majority should come as no surprise in our business-driven culture. (Economic determinism, the pundits call it.) Pressing for profit, consumed by consumerism, enmeshed in materialism, most people in our society are maximalists. They want more – not less – of anything deemed to have value: more money, more goods, more fun, more . . . make your own list.

For maximalists, less is not more; less is less. And since, in their minds, only more is more, more is more desirable than less, which is less desirable. However, from the minimalist perspective, if less is more, the more less you have, the more you have.

But more (rather than less) to the point, what makes less more in the minds of minimalists are the benefits of simplicity and refinement, benefits that are visual, aesthetic, spatial, and, perhaps, even spiritual.

Minimalism eschews clutter: no frills, no frivolous ornamentation, no superfluous accessorization. From the minimalist point of view, a room filled with furniture, for example, looks like a window display in a furniture store. A room with one solitary piece of furniture, on the other hand, appears artful and intriguing. Having less in a room means having more space, more light, more air, which are probably the only "mores" that are good in minimalism.

Open-plan home design, of which the loft is a prime example, is a minimalist concept (and, in the minds of some, a radical idea). There are no – or few – inside walls to carve up the space and obstruct the view. Without cubicles, without barriers, the space is dispersed. Without visual impediments, without corners, the result is a sort of transparency, a kind of endless depth that is accompanied by constant rediscovery of aspects of the space, which you experience from wherever you happen to sit or stand at any particular moment. A line. A shadow. The play of light.

There's always something different for the eye to enjoy.

Without walls, the space is, in essence, one big room. With no walls to define the inner space, the functions of various areas of the one big room are defined by their contents. Where the sofa sits is the living room. Where the dining table sits is the dining room. Where the bed sits is the bedroom. Where the owner sits is wherever there's a chair. Without fixed, concrete boundaries, the loosely defined spaces are flexible, expandable (also expendable), movable, switchable.

However, as we later discovered, it's hard to live in absolute minimalism. If you have books, for example, you need bookcases. If you have guests, you need seats. If you have a life, you need the artifacts of living: furniture, appliances, utensils. And when you get them, you have to put them somewhere. And when you put enough of them somewhere, you achieve what is popularly known as an accumulation, or worse yet, an overaccumulation. Yes, or even maximalism.

Though still determined minimalists in theory, we've had to make compromises. Currently, my office, I confess, is a prime example of the clutter I've inveighed against. It's about as maximalist as a space can get, exceeding even the shambles in our TV-room-cum-library. If Colleen had her way, my office would be declared a disaster area. I can only say in defence that it's not a total loss. At least it looks out over a minimalist living room. Well, sort of minimalist.

So there we were at last, where all our accumulated next moves had led us, fretting over what was now an empty box. And still no blasted permit. While we marked time, mulling over the drawings with Richard and wandering impatiently around the emptiness our wreckers had delivered, the framing was put on hold, pending arrival of the permit. Frank, the carpenter, and his helpers, Nick and Dominic, were standing by. What to do? We'd lose them if we didn't start.

Once again, we stuck our necks out and gave them the go-ahead. They started. And that's precisely when the inspector walked back in, screamed bloody murder, got really ugly (he wasn't that good looking to begin with), and closed us down again. Two days later, we heard from city hall. The permit was ready. Come and get it.

We'd already paid for the permit months before. Now all we had to do was pick it up. But Richard had been warned that when we did, we would, in some manner not made explicit, be penalized for jumping the gun. Expecting something punitive but relatively minor, Colleen went for the permit.

She arrived at city hall at 11:30 in the morning and was told that the clerk who handled permits was off for lunch. No one else could deal with it. (Well, it's city hall, right?) So Colleen waited.

At one o'clock the clerk returned, the remains of his lunch on his moustache – all indications were that he'd had some-thing with mustard and relish – and advised Colleen that, on the instructions of his superiors, as a penalty for our mis-demeanours we were being assessed an additional amount equal to the not inconsiderable fee we'd already paid for the permit. In other words, because of our impatience at being held up, we had to pay double for the permit. Double! Colleen was speechless. What was there to say? The clerk was merely a messenger, just doing his job. Besides, though driven to our misbehaviour by the delay at city hall, we were legally, technically, and morally in the wrong. We broke the rules. Mea culpa.

I guess what we learned – again – is that you can't fight city hall. Cheque or credit card. Either will be fine. Thank you. Have a good day.

CHAPTER 8

A HOUSE RISES IN THE RUINS

The loft saga could now continue legally. In addition to the extensive framing of our big empty space, there was all the standard work that went into constructing a home: carpentry, wiring, plumbing, ductwork, drywall, masonry, concrete. But due to the nature and scale of our renovation, none of these could be handled in the standard way. Heating and cooling and soundproofing, in particular, posed special problems, and the framing had to be designed to make allowances for them.

Framing is in many ways the most important step in building because it undergirds most of the later construction. If the framing is not right, it will come back years later to haunt you. The framer's challenge is to construct a skeleton of wood, or to use the sculptor's term, an armature, to which everything else is fastened, and which it supports. Obviously, the framing has to be strong enough to bear the weight it will carry for who knows how many lifetimes: floors, walls, and roofs plus all the things that go on to floors, walls, and roofs. And that isn't all there is to it. For horizontal surfaces to be level and vertical surfaces not to lean, measurement must be precise because the framing has to be square and exact. And the wood that goes into the framing can't be green; it has to be kiln-dried and free of imperfections so that it doesn't at some future date warp and twist and crack and craze and let the building – and its startled inhabitants – down. Clearly, framing is important in new construction. But it was especially important in our project since we were, in effect, building a new building inside an old building, a house within a house.

Framing is a specialty. Not all carpenters are framing carpenters. We were fortunate that our lost contractor had recommended an Old World master carpenter, who was not only an excellent framer but also a highly skilled finishing carpenter and cabinetmaker. In Frank, who was the first tradesman to set foot on our project, we had a real find. He didn't let us down. And neither did his framing.

In executing Richard's precise plans for the framing of the exterior walls, Frank had to veer from conventional practice, so that the entire inside of the building could be clad in a continuous vapour barrier of unbroken plastic. To maintain the integrity of the insulation and keep heating

A house rises in the ruins. Once again, alliteration saves the day. Alternatively, "a house within a house" where the save is made by repetition.

*In effect, we were building a house inside a house. Above: Still a lot to do. Below: A little less to do.
That's the author on the ladder.*

The Urban Loft

High block wall stabilized with wooden beam and framed in and ready for drywall. When the beam looked unattractive, Richard hid it with drywall.

High on the now finished block wall in the living room, Colleen's banners, "Thirteen Ways of Looking at a Blackbird,"
based on the poem by Wallace Stevens.

and cooling costs down, Richard had specified that this barrier have no holes in it and no patches. And Frank helped make it happen. Where necessary, to avoid punching through the plastic and breaking the vapour barrier, the electrical wiring did not go into the outside walls but into a specially designed conduit or chase built by Frank into a ledge around the outside wall.

Frank was very conscientious about the fact that the vapour barrier was sacrosanct. But this fact had to be constantly reinforced to the other tradespeople who were used to the conventional practice of punching holes in the plastic and then patching the rips with tape. It was an

A birdless cage in a choirless loft. Eiffel, isn't it? The raven on the ledge in the background is not in the cage, merely contemplating it.

ongoing battle to have it done our way. In any renovation, there is always conflict between conventional and unconventional practice.

To preserve Richard's open plan vision, Frank framed the loft with only a few dividing walls. Dividing walls couldn't, however, be entirely avoided since the floor of the mezzanine level was to be built on top of them. The few inside walls that were built on the main floor and on the mezzanine were designed to hide ductwork, provide built-in storage, hang paintings, and display art objects, while creating as few barriers as possible.

Elsewhere in the building, the framing also had to accommodate a number of Drdla-designed intricacies. The best example of this was his design of the entry hall with its various levels artfully laid out to delay exposing the scale of the inner space to visitors as they come into the building. When Richard decided to replace the old entry stairs, he took a kind of Alfred Hitchcock approach to the design to heighten the suspense of entry. Richard makes you wait . . . wait . . . wait . . . And then, at the very last moment, he lets you have it. The volume you see when you reach the top of the stairs is so unexpected it's a shock. Even for us.

Where walls were unavoidable, "windows" in the drywall open the space up and provide convenient sills for things to sit on like this birdless cage.

The Urban Loft

In addition to the framing, another architectural element played a major role in our renovation. This was the unusually large concrete-block demising wall separating the two halves of the church. Building it was a formidable project for a number of reasons. Size, for one. Starting in the basement, the wall rises fifty feet to the roof and runs thirty-seven-and-a-half feet across the church. The size and purpose of the wall posed some engineering problems. With little attached to the wall on either side, what would stabilize this high structure? On the advice of a consulting mechanical engineer, the wall was reinforced on our side with a multi-layered wooden beam running right across it about eight feet below the ceiling.

In addition, the wall had to be soundproof. Airborne sound needs a barrier of dense, heavy material to prevent its transmission. The concrete-block construction of the wall would take care of that. Structural sound needs a barrier of air to stop it. Cutting the floor between the two halves of the church and leaving a gap for air down the middle of the wall between the layers of block would accomplish this. There would be almost no transmission of sound through the wall. In addition, for fire protection, the code required insulation and drywall on at least one side of the wall, which would provide some further acoustical benefit.

Inside the old entry hall. It suffers from a certain lack of excitement. Note the transom window above the doors, now removed.

The cost of insulating and drywalling one side of the great divide was shared equally, but would result in the loss of three inches of floor space to the side on which the material was applied. We flipped a coin with our neighbours to decide which side would gain the drywall and lose the inches. We won the toss. And our gracious neighbours accepted the loss, taking the insulation and drywall on their side and leaving us the extra three inches and the exposed block wall, a look we preferred.

This, however, also left the supportive wooden beam exposed on our side of the wall. Running eight feet below the ceiling, it appeared strangely unattractive up there. Richard contrived to have the beam cunningly hidden under a drywall overlap of the upper wall. He also came up with a simple but brilliant idea for the exposed block. In a normal exposed-block wall, the mortar pattern is rectangular like the building blocks themselves. But Richard found blocks for us that had a mortar-like groove down the centre so that when put in place, a square mortar pattern emerged that fit in with the pattern which became a theme in many other details of our plan.

In building the wall, we planned to divide and conquer. But the actual construction of the wall turned out to be piecemeal pandemonium. Because of the delays bemoaned

The new entrance hall seen from above. We would greet visitors from here but you can't do that and open the door at the same time.

The Urban Loft

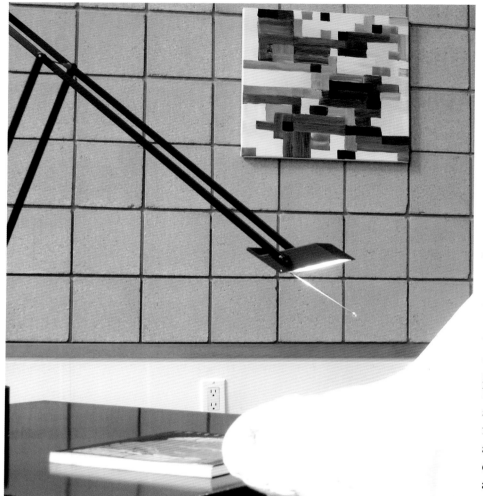

"Noise" painted by Canadian artist Richard Storms picks up the theme of square mortar pattern of the block wall.

fortunately not erratically – until the monumental job was completed. Needless to say, it took longer than it should have and therefore cost more than it should have.

And then, one magical day, the wall was finished and towered above us. Emissaries were sent to the other side of the wall to shout and scream and bellow and raise a clamour and make all manner of disturbance as a test of the mighty structure's acoustic impermeability. All that we heard on our side was the sound of mortar drying, which is akin to silence. And it was good. And we were pleased. And there has been silence between the two halves of the divided church ever since. Amen. (If only other divided churches were that peaceful.)

Richard's design was simple, clean, contemporary. No frills. No foolishness. And certainly no baseboards, no moulding. But getting the design executed without the baseboards met with all sorts of resistance and gave us no end of grief. In the end, we made a compromise. Instead of conventional baseboards, the drywall was detailed to end in a recessed return about three inches above the floor and a black board was set in to the wall underneath the return. This treatment is used in office buildings all the time. It was in the specifications. The drywall contractor had quoted it that way. No problem, he had said. Yet his installers insisted it couldn't be done as per the specs.

The result was an ongoing argument with the installers in our attempt to get the drywall done as designed. To make matters worse, one of the installers ranted all day about the "rotten job" and how he wasn't being paid enough. It drove the other drywallers up the wall they were drywalling. The mouth never shut up, wailing constantly, except for when the boss was on the site.

earlier concerning the permit, we had lost our block-layer and could find no one to replace him. It was a busy period in the industry and everybody, it seemed, was booked up. In order to get our wall built, we had to seduce the block-layers who were working on the condos in the church hall next door. By paying them a premium for the work, we were able to convince them to moonlight on our job whenever they could fit us in. Many people had a hand in our great wall (and in our pockets). The wall rose sporadically – but

The stairs watched by a metal bird perched in drywall window. Metal birds spare us bird droppings. But rust may be in the wings.

The Urban Loft

From Colleen's vast collection of personally painted, colour coded doors, a small selection.
Green – furnace room. Red – laundry room. Marigold – main bathroom. Blue – garage.

One day, adding injury to insult, the drywall contractor himself, who was pitching in and carrying a sheet of drywall, fell off the floor of the mezzanine and into the stairwell. He wouldn't have fallen if the safety railing had been in place. The safety railing wasn't in place because the mouthy installer had removed it and neglected to replace it. Though no bones were broken, the contractor was badly banged up, extensively bruised, and in considerable pain. He could have fallen down three floors into the basement. Fortunately, he escaped that fate by hanging onto the sheet of drywall that he was carrying when he fell. The fall didn't break the drywall but the drywall did break his fall, for which we were all truly grateful.

To make matters worse, the inspectors walked in on the drywallers one day to find them working on stilts rather than on the scaffold. Not at our behest, I might add. Working on stilts may be faster, but can be dangerous. Years ago, stilts were common. Today, for safety reasons, they're not permitted. The inspectors raised the roof and lowered the boom. As a penalty, they shut the drywalling down for three days.

Finally, after much squabbling with, and among, the drywallers, the job of drywalling was finished. The only problem was that it wasn't finished. The returns had not been done as designed. They would have to be redone. But we'd had enough aggravation. Sick of the hassle, tired of arguing, and eager to see the last of the troublesome drywallers, we paid off the drywall contractor in full, as per his quote. Then we got someone else in, at our additional cost, to redo the faulty drywall returns.

Despite all our aggravation, a couple of weeks later the

*The stairs seen from the living room. And everywhere openings – between the treads, in the walls, in the drywall.
With all those openings, we should be hiring.*

drywall contractor called Richard, pleading with him for additional money. He believed he was owed more than the amount he had quoted and had already been paid. He'd taken a bath on this job, he argued with Richard, because of our insistence on the bottom return detail, which he now claimed – incorrectly – hadn't been in the original job specifications. Could we help him out with the extra money that he felt was coming to him? Richard told him several times we couldn't.

Then the drywall contractor called me directly and asked for more money. I wasn't sure what to do. The drywallers had given us a great deal of grief. I explained to him that I had a bill in front of me for redoing his incomplete drywall job. If he'd pay that bill, I'd pay him the extra money he wanted. How much was the bill? he asked. I told him. It was very close to the extra amount he was after. Silence on the other end of the line. Then he said, "I guess you won't help me out then?" I said I was sorry.

TALES FROM THE TRADES

Another significant architectural element in our project, and yet another major undertaking, was the windows. The four original windows in the living room area in our part of the church were in two pairs facing north. Tall but narrow, they didn't let in much light, even after the removal of the stained glass. To get more north light into the building, we decided to knock out the brickwork between each pair of windows, creating two five-and-a-half-foot-wide window openings out of the four narrower ones. In addition, by lowering the sills, the height of the window openings would be extended to fifteen feet. For these enlarged openings, and with a little input from us, Richard designed two very handsome industrial-type thermal windows. Framed on the exterior in striking matte black aluminum, they picked up the square grid motif established by the blocks in the demising wall.

The windows, of course, had to be custom made. Need I say they were costly?

As we learned daily, everything about property renovation is costly. Of church conversions, it might be said that costliness is next to godliness. Or maybe it's the other way around.

After the windows were fabricated, the two immense, heavy, double-glazed units were delivered on a flatbed truck that filled our little street. It took a crew with a crane to install the monsters. Half the street (the openly curious half) came out to watch the operation. From behind closed curtains and drawn drapes, the other half watched the watchers watching.

When the windows were delivered, we discovered scratches on the black frames, which, from their pattern, had to have happened during their manufacture. We agreed to let the workmen proceed with the installation and solve the problem later. The fabricators offered us a choice of two options as compensation. They would give us a discount on the price of the windows and leave them as they were. (Which would have meant, at some future time, having to repaint the frames.) Or, if we preferred, they would cover the scratched metal frames with a thin cladding of unsullied black metal. Since the

To let in light, four narrow windows have been made into two huge windows by bashing out the brickwork. Quite a bash, followed by rubble.

A one window inside view of the living room from behind the sofa. That's my office on the mezzanine glowing softly overhead.

The Urban Loft

Looking down – but not condescendingly – at Richard's ziggurat bookcase nestled between the windows.

windows were a major visual feature in the loft, we opted for perfection and chose the second avenue. We did the right thing. The windows were – and still are – spectacular. They needed to be perfect.

The window frames are matte black on the outside and silver gray on the inside. The finished windows are augmented inside by wide, handsome maple window seats with a central wooden grid over heating and air conditioning vents. Screened, crank-open widow panes within the big windows swing out to let outside air in, when desired.

These giant windows, striking in the geometry of their design, have never had drapes or blinds put on them. Hanging like Mondrian paintings on our north wall, they are too beautiful to cover.

This was pretty radical stuff in an area where people keep their windows covered night and day, blinds down, drapes drawn. I often wonder, if windows are covered twenty-four hours a day, what's the point of having the windows? Maybe the point is just to have something to cover. After all, without windows, where would you put your blinds and your drapes?

Let me add one last thing connected with our wonderful windows. I'm jumping ahead, but one incredibly cold winter night, just after we'd moved into the church, a funny thing happened. Colleen, who was home alone, was startled when the unlocked front door opened and in walked three men, faces

The world outside as seen through our birdcage and one of the big windows.

Dining room with open doors (windows, actually, with door handles) that let you step out to the ground floor deck. Or you can dine and look out.

covered in black balaclavas. This scary moment was prolonged by the fact that the masked trio, assuming that Colleen expected them, didn't explain who they were or why they were there.

Colleen was, in fact, expecting the repair people who were coming to put the cladding on the scratched window frames. And that's who the ominous visitors turned out to be. However, Colleen wasn't expecting them at

53

Looking in one of the big windows at night. Spectacular, intriguing, yet remarkably private.
This kind of design could put makers of drapes out of business.

The Urban Loft

seven o'clock at night, nor was she expecting them to appear in black balaclavas. And the masked men, balaclavas frosting over, worked late into the night, making the repairs despite the temperature. No problem, ma'am. We're used to it. We work outside all year round. Come to think of it, so do the windows.

Good natural light had always been a vital component in our search for the ideal space. The church would have plenty of natural light during the day; we were now faced with decisions about artificial light. How were we to light the loft at night?

Lighting, already an art unto itself and highly subjective, had been made even more complex – and sometimes problematical – by low-voltage technology. Despite this, we'd long been hot on halogens, the little quartz bulbs that, with the help of transformers, operated on twelve volts. We liked their bright, white light; their smallness, their minimalism. We liked the engineered, high-tech look of the fixtures they plugged into. Early on, we had decided our haven would be halogen lit. And mostly, it is.

Strikingly bright and dramatic, halogen lighting was not without its dark side. For inexplicable reasons, the compact mini-transformers that run them repeatedly burned out and had

Hanging like Mondrian paintings on the north wall, the giant windows are too beautiful to cover. Besides, we don't have to. You can't really see in.

The living room comes into view at the top of the stairs just past Colleen's three-dimensional "Walking Man".
If the art doesn't stop you, the view will.

The Urban Loft

55

to be replaced. If the transformers were the fusible type, the fuses burned out and had to be replaced. Neither repair was convenient. The first was expensive, and both usually required an electrician, at least for people like us who are easily shocked. During our first year in the church, our lighting equipment supplier generously replaced virtually all our transformers without cost, attributing their early demise to manufacturing deficiencies. Quality control. Where did it go?

The halogen bulbs were themselves quick to flame out, despite their high price, fancy packaging, and manufacturer's claims of longevity. The little twenty-watt bi-pins were particularly touchy. If you inadvertently touched the glass, skin oils made the bulbs burn out almost instantly. As Richard taught me, the trick is to handle halogens with rubber gloves.

Worse, the receptacles that accept the bi-pins seemed to corrode or degenerate in the immense heat, twisting and warping out of shape until they finally refused to accept replacement bulbs, or broke the pins off if you tried to force the bulbs to fit. When that happened, the fixtures had to be replaced, a procedure that again involved an electrician.

The wiring in our latter-day lighthouse is extensive, endless, requiring miles of wire for our many lights, plus more miles of multicoloured spaghetti for our utilities. Though we have a gas furnace, gas hot water tank, and gas cooktop, they all require electricity to operate. In the gas furnace, electricity

The snake pit, a profusion of wiring. Plus all the wireless stuff. In a power blackout, we're toast. Or maybe just bread.

powers the ignition system, the fan, the thermostat, and various other controls I have yet to learn about and don't want to know about too soon. The gas hot water heater uses electrical power to operate the motor in its circulating system. And, of course, the burners on our gas cooktop are ignited by spark plugs, which are powered by electricity. All of the above require wires, wires, wires.

Also at the end of one electrical wire or another are the humidifier; the electronic air cleaner; the air conditioner; the central vac; the various exhaust fans in the kitchen, laundryroom, bathrooms, and attic; and the fan in the high-level hot air return. Add to this all our other kitchen and laundry appliances and all my office and computer gear and you can see why the electrical board in our basement looks like a snakepit. And I'm not even going to mention all the telephone wires leading from the two outside phone lines to seven phones, and a fax machine and a modem, or the countless – who knows how many? – other future-use outlets on four levels. And, of course, there was all the cable TV stuff for a single, lonely TV set, which we rarely watch but for which we pay monthly tribute so that we can access the occasional worthwhile program, if we can remember when it's on.

Most of our wiring, though not all, was done by a competent young electrician in the employ of an electrical contracting company owned by his father. Father was usually busy else-

Detail of window frames in library-cum-TV room. Nuts and bolts treatment and paint job by Colleen. Crocadog on sill, a gift from our kids.

A quiet corner amongst the books in the library-cum-TV room. Shh! I'm trying to read.

The Urban Loft

The master bedroom, our most successful room in terms of our minimalist intentions.

where. He only came around if there was a problem, or to pick up a cheque. The young electrician – though qualified, capable, and hard working – fell short in two respects.

First, like many tradesmen, he'd never worked with an architect before (especially not one who also managed the trades). He didn't understand that he was responsible to the architect. Unlike Frank, who at Richard's request respected the vapour barrier, the electric-kid kept wanting to punch holes through the plastic. When Richard corrected him, the electrician took his case to Colleen, who, had no idea whatsoever about wiring and referred him back to Richard. But the young electrician simply failed to communicate with the architect. There was a short circuit there somewhere.

The other thing about this electrical whiz was that like many sub-contractors, he kept disappearing to other projects and we never knew when, or if, he was coming back. This in itself was no surprise. All the sub-contractors did this to us in varying degrees. But about three-quarters of the way through our job, the wire jockey took off to another project and, perhaps in a snit about not getting his way, never came back. After we gave up trying to track him down and get him back, we had no choice but to find someone else to finish the wiring.

High level hot air returns shine in the early morning winter sunlight coming through the clerestory. These pipes recycle heat and reduce heating bills.

And, of course, when the electrical work was all finished, who showed up but Father, seeking a cheque for the large balance he believed was owing for add-on work done by his son. After some delay and debate, Richard was finally able to sit Father down and go through the work list with him, detailing what was done and what wasn't, to determine what was actually owed.

Some items on the list were included in the original contract and others his son simply had not done. Once he was made aware of the details, Father, who hadn't heard the whole story, revised his figures and apologized for his son. "You have to excuse him," he said. "He's just a kid."

Not all our sub-contractors were young, of course. And some were more grown-up than others. Denham, our heating and air conditioning contractor, for example, was very

Looking towards the bedroom from the hall. In any direction, there's always something interesting for the eye to light on. It's one photo op after another.

state of the art systems. The pollution-reducing, high-efficiency furnace, for example, doesn't have a chimney. It doesn't need a chimney because it doesn't emit smoke. It emits only a little water vapour, which is vented through a small duct on the back wall.

Managing the airflow is the key to the efficiency of the heating and cooling system. The system's circulating fan was designed to be kept running year round. It is never turned off, except for servicing. Whatever the season, this fan circulates the air and helps keep the temperature uniform throughout the large space. With no hot or cold spots to skew temperature readings, this enables the thermostat to deliver accurately what it promises.

For the cold winter months, we installed a high-level hot air return system, consisting of two huge, very industrial looking, round metal ducts that run up the walls to within inches of our living room ceiling. The ducts draw in the heated air that has risen to ceiling level, recycling it back into the heating system, where it is reheated and recirculated. The resulting fuel savings are considerable. Despite the above average volume of our loft, our gas costs for heating, hot water, and cooking are less than for the average home.

Our air conditioning also does an efficient job of cooling our difficult-to-cool space. While the cost of cooling is not as reasonable as the cost of heating, it is still about the same as the cost of cooling a large home.

We were so pleased with the guys who installed all this stuff that we've retained them on a service contract ever since. Their ongoing maintenance service, three times a

grown-up. An African-American of imposing height and build, he had come to Canada as a professional football player. When his playing days were over, he had stayed on and gone into the hot and cold business. That his venture had thrived was a testament not only to the big guy's competence and drive but also to his engaging manner, which seemed to have been passed on to all the people he employed.

Not only were these guys pleasant to do business with, they did an outstanding job of fulfilling specifications for the heating and air conditioning; no small achievement when you consider the huge volumes of air involved.

After seeking advice from a consulting engineer, Richard worked with Denham to come up with some innovative, year, continues to be first rate, just like the work they did on the installation.

Another of the sub-trades that was above par was John, by training a plumber but actually a small contractor with many skills. He, too, was a former athlete. A tall, thin, Henry Fonda kind of guy, the one-time hockey player from the Maritimes was one of the mainstays of the project. Along with Frank, John was on the job throughout, hired as both plumbing and painting contractor. John, in addition to his other duties and un-asked, appointed himself Friday night clean-up person. He just couldn't bring himself to leave a mess behind when he went home for the weekend.

Despite wearing many hats, John was never in a hurry to get paid. We used to have to pester him to present us with periodic bills. Even then, he only did so reluctantly – indeed, almost apologetically.

John had some old industrial shelving sitting in his backyard not doing anything. When he found out we were planning to put some storage in the furnace room, he insisted on giving us his shelving. He delivered it, assembled it, installed it, and refused to take payment for it. After much nagging, which I'm quite good at, we got him to accept in return a revolving storage car-ousel with a mirror on it. He had admired this item and had offered to buy it when he learned that we had decided to dispose of it because it didn't suit our plans.

The plumbing in a structure the size of the church had to cover a lot of ground; shut-off valves and cut-off taps were put in all over the place to handle emergencies. The trouble was that in an emergency, a non-plumber would never know what they were. John very thoughtfully took the trouble of putting a little round string tag on each of them, identifying what each was for. This in itself was not so unusual. But what was unusual – yet so typical of the man – was that it had occurred to him that the airflow

might cause the string tags to turn; they were not always within easy reach to be turned around. To overcome this, he took the trouble to write the identifying information on both sides of the tags. A small thing. But a big thing. Sometimes, less is more. Sometimes more is more.

John painting the stairwell. Note ziggurat drywall detail. Drywall is basically boring. A ziggurat puts a little zip into your drywall. Art also works.

CHAPTER 10

THE KITCHEN

The kitchen, it has been said, probably by a cardiologist who likes to cook, is the heart of the home. I wouldn't argue. It's where all the food is stored. It's where all the meals are prepared. It's where everybody seems to want to hang out when you're having a party.

The kitchen is also the message centre of the home. Just look at all that stuff up on the refrigerator door. Without a kitchen, how would we keep in touch with each other? How would we communicate? Without a refrigerator, where would we put our fridge magnets?

Kitchens seem to fall into two broad categories. There's the real-life kitchen, the one you've got – the make-do kitchen. And then, there's the make-believe kitchen, the dream kitchen touted in the media, the really well-designed food preparation centre that everyone claims to aspire to; the work saving, time saving, step saving, practical, beautiful configuration that's a joy to be in, and a treat to work in.

The dream kitchen is a feature in every home magazine, in every weekend newspaper, and on every television cooking show. Everyone talks about the dream kitchen. No one talks about the dream bedroom or the dream dining room or the dream living room. The dream is about the kitchen. And unless you're doing a major makeover or building from scratch, you rarely get an opportunity to attempt to build a dream kitchen.

We had that rare opportunity. After many meetings with us, Richard devised a layout that included a centre island with lots of storage, lots of counter space, and lots of room to work. This was going to be a thoughtfully configured kitchen. Two of the counter tops would be granite. We shopped for them and picked them out ourselves (although we couldn't pick them up ourselves). The top of the centre island would be an elongated oval of solid, butcher-block maple. It would be custom made by a small northern Ontario woodworking shop that specialized in solid maple products, which they ship all over the continent. (Except for ours, which was shipped directly to us.)

Leaving nothing to chance, we planned to have the kitchen cabinets assembled by kitchen cabinet specialists. With Richard's advice, and drawings in hand, we shopped around at half a

Frank carpentering our kitchen dining room pass through bar, while Satch supervises the work. Both performed excellently in their respective roles.

The pass through, as seen from the dining room, lets you stay in contact with the kitchen while dining, without having to use e-mail.

63

The kitchen's maple block centre island is durable, long lasting and there for us meal after meal.
Hence the patriotic song, "The Maple Block Forever".

An end view of the centre island. Who says there's no end to kitchen photography?

dozen kitchen shops and discovered first-hand why so few homes have dream kitchens. Dream kitchens are nightmarishly expensive.

After getting quotes from three of the kitchen specialists, we chose the middle bid, (a) because we liked the sales rep with whom we were dealing and, (b) because we worried that if we accepted the lowest bid, it might mean corners would be cut, to our later regret. And speaking of later regret, we'd later regret choosing the bid we chose.

Having avoided – we thought – the obvious risk inherent in the low bid, we then encountered other risks not yet catalogued in the International Compendium of Designer

Looking over the range top, through the pass through and towards the block wall with the shirts on it is better than television.

Kitchen Risks – problems we could never have imagined.

Everything that could possibly go wrong did. The sales rep we liked fell ill. Or so we were told. As a result, he was away from work for several weeks. Then, when he got well, did he come back to work? No, sir, he did not. He left the company for a job with another kitchen cabinet maker. Which one? The one that had given us the high bid. Perhaps our rep's illness had been highly contagious PDS (pre-departure sickness). We'll never know. In any event, we were left in kitchen cabinet limbo.

From the dining room table through the pass through into the kitchen; the view also captures the eye and tickles the palate.

Here the view from the dining room through the kitchen and along the hall takes your eye to the painting hanging just outside the powder room.

Not one but two views: the pass through on the left, the living room on the right. What a deal!

To complicate matters, our chosen kitchen experts got into some sort of financial problem, or so it appeared. The exact nature of the difficulty was never revealed to us. Following that, the company either changed ownership or went into receivership. Suddenly, we were talking to new people who had no idea what our project was all about. For all we knew, they could have been the receivers.

Amazingly, despite all this confusion, the cabinets were completed and delivered and installed . . . and deficient. Maple trim was missing in some places. Things didn't fit in other places. The under-the-sink cabinet was constructed in a way that didn't provide the space required for the large

Up close on our Parsons table in the dining room. We've had it for 25 years and it still stands up when we sit down at it.

sink we had gone to great pains to find. In the end, to avoid the major expense of deconstructing and reconstructing the under-the-sink cabinet, we had to return the large sink and settle for a smaller one.

We voiced our dissatisfaction, of course. And four dark-suited executive types, who had just bought either the suits or the company, came to inspect the installation and lend an ear to our complaints. Nodding promisingly in all the right places, they listened. And, still nodding, they left. And you can guess what they did.

While we debated our options, I got an unexpected call from someone I didn't know. He identified himself as another unsatisfied customer of our kitchen cabinet suppliers. Had we been satisfied with the job they'd done? Before I'd give him any information, I wanted to know how he'd gotten my phone number. He explained that he was very unhappy with the job done on his kitchen. When the company sent someone to assess his complaint, our complainant had peeked at a list of customers on a clipboard the inspector had put down. There, he spotted and jotted my name and number.

Yes, I confided to the spotter and jotter, I was a fellow sufferer. We, too, were unhappy. That's what he had wanted to confirm, he told me. He was planning to sue the kitchen cabinet people and suggested I might want to do the same. I told him I was averse to litigation, didn't want to go to court, didn't want to get into a hassle. I had ample hassles

The kitchen communication centre. Fridge magnets at work, supporting our children and grandchildren.

aplenty and didn't need more. Good luck with your problem. I'll solve mine some other way. Thanks for your call and have yourself a good lawsuit.

We wound up solving the problem the same way we solved all the problems that dogged the church renovation. It's called: pay more. Fortunately, good old reliable Frank was able, at additional cost and with Richard's guidance, to saw out, chisel out, plane out, or hammer out most of the kitchen problems, with the exception of the under-the-sink cabinet.

The kitchen is spacious, a good working layout around a centre island – of maple, of course – with lots of metal in the side-by-side gas cooktop and electric grill, topped by a metal exhaust hood and bottomed by big metal storage racks. There are also two granite counters, under-hanging cabinets with more storage in them and storage cabinets below, as well. The red floor covering is rubber. It comes in 40" by 40" square sheets. It's easy to care for and easy on the cook's feet. The two floor-to-ceiling kitchen closets – one is a pantry, one holds cleaning supplies – with doors painted many coats of bright marigold by Colleen, not only brighten up the room and make it look sunny but also store tons of stuff.

So that's our dream kitchen. And we enjoy it. But I have a confession to make. Once you attempt to cook in a dream kitchen, you realize there really is no such thing. A dream is just a dream.

THE CHOIRLESS LOFT

lthough the renovation entailed a major transformation of the church space, we decided, in little random acts of creative anachronism (i.e., whimsy), to save a few things that we felt might serve as modest mementos of the building's past, without being incongruous in the new minimalist aesthetic we had imposed on the building.

The hanging lights, which had been removed from the church ceiling, had been stored in the basement till we decided what to do with them. There were four of these striking, hexagonal lamps in our half of the church. About two feet in length, each of these silver-gray cast aluminum fixtures held six etched glass panes.

Each lamp had been suspended from six short chains leading to a long central chain that went up to the ceiling.

We shortened the chains and installed two lamps in the ceiling of our entrance hall, where they now greet our guests. We hung a third from the ceiling of our bedroom where, quite by chance, it can be seen from the street through our front windows, giving passersby pause, or pleasure, or both. A fourth lamp, turned upside down, and with the chains removed, became an unusual but practical end table in our living room.

Another item we rescued from the church was a wall painting. High on the walls and close to the ceiling all around the old church had run a series of large, round, mosaic medallions depicting scenes of biblical significance. In the course of the renovation, the tiles that made up these medallions were removed, and we discovered that each configuration of tiles had been cemented over an earlier painting. While these simple underpaintings may not have been fine art, some were very interesting, and one or two stood out.

One that particularly caught our fancy was located in what turned out to be our bedroom. It was on the wall just above our newly replaced bedroom window. Encircled in an ornate, gray ring, on a pale green background, a dove hovered over seven tongues of fire. Time and tile cement wait for no man, and both had taken their toll. The colours were faded and weak. The paint had come away in a couple of places. The painting felt, somehow, like an ancient relic found

The underpainting, saved after the mosaic tiles were removed, may have been meant as a guide for the tiles that were cemented over it.

One of the saved church lamps now hangs over our bed. It's one of the few inside things that can be seen from the street.

The bedroom art collection: one of the saved church lamps, the saved underpainting over the window and Colleen's painting, "Embarkation".

on an archeological dig. Which, of course, it wasn't; it had probably been painted in 1940 or 1941. Still, it appealed to us for aesthetic rather than religious reasons. We decided that we would like to preserve the painting.

While all the other underpaintings were to be covered by drywall, or otherwise obscured in the construction, this one was to be spared and remain visible. Richard designed the framing around the painted area in such a way as to exempt it from coverage by insulation and drywalling. This exception was carefully explained to the drywallers. The wall over the window was specifically framed to leave the painting uncovered by drywall.

Are you listening, dryguys? No drywall goes on this section of the wall. We want the painting to show. Understand?

For once, the drywallers were listening; they understood and did precisely as they were bidden. They drywalled around the painting, instead of over it. No drywall obscured the painting. Unhidden, unobstructed, the painting was there in full view, for all to see. What a relief. Finally, we were doing something right. But it was not to last.

When the drywallers had finished their work in the bedroom, the tapers came in and taped the joints, and then plastered them over with the "mud" (i.e., drywall compound) they use. After the mud dried, it was sanded smooth so that no seams showed. But while the tapers were plastering mud

The not yet famous "Confetti Chair" created by Colleen on a much-recycled armchair.

Our two door entrance with one door open for people. For elephants. we open both doors.

maple floor revealed after we finally ripped up the ancient torn carpeting and the cracked linoleum under that. But there was a surprise when the altar was taken out. Where the altar had been there was no floor to save, but only a hole. It shouldn't have been a surprise, of course. It stands to reason, after all, that under an altar you would find a holy floor. Still, for us, the unholy, who planned to live there, the hole in the floor would have to be patched. And later, it was, with the old maple flooring our next-door neighbours were kind enough to give us, reclaimed from the dismantling of the choir loft in their half of the church.

After the floor was patched, it was restored, sanded, and treated with emollients to preserve its complexion. It looks like what it is, an old floor saved. We like the look of it. We don't wax it. We just damp mop it, once in a while. Lightly. And we have it oiled every three or four years with a mixture of tung oil and varnish – I'm not sure what tung oil is either – which preserves the wood and gives it that warm, golden colour.

Saved, as well, were the double doors with little leaded windows in them, which were the old side entrance of the church. These doors became our front entrance, though we use only one of them. We keep the other one locked, opening it only to bring through something wide. Like an elephant or an army tank. This only happens a couple of times a year, during zoo meetings or military exercises.

The doors were made of sturdy oak but they were somewhat ravaged by weather and time. We got Frank to carpenter away their deficiencies, rebuild the doorframe, and rehang the doors, which now sport brushed stainless steel hardware. We got a leaded glass craftsman to come in and repair the broken leading in one of the windows, which we wanted to preserve. Finally, we painted the dual portals black. Like the hair I used to have before the conversion of the church, only darker.

on the joints, they also plastered mud over the rescued painting, totally obliterating it.

When we discovered this the next day, Richard made the tapers remove the hardened mud from the painting. No easy task. It had to be soaked and washed and eased off. This took its toll, further degrading the colours in the painting and removing more patches of paint. But by this point, we were absolutely determined to have the painting, no matter what. Colleen had said that she might take a brush to it and try to restore it. But it didn't happen. We seem to like it just as it is.

We were also able, as we had hoped, to save the grungy

Fastened to the wall under the window seats, the perforated metal echoes the stair railings and accents the maple / metal connection.

CHAPTER 12

MOVING DAY AND WHAT CAME AFTER

S peaking of dark things, let me reiterate that the church renovation began while we were still living in that darkest of all places, the rented condo apartment. But in a trice, or maybe a trice and a half, tempus was, as the Romans might have said, fugiting. We had leased the mondo condo for a year. Before you could say, "Presto change-o, reno," our year in the gloom was up, over, finished. The lease was about to run out. And at the church, we still had "miles to go before we sleep." What was our next move to be?

We'd bought the church in August of 1993. Renovation – delayed and sporadic – had started in November of that year and was still going on over Easter of 1994. It seemed to be taking forever. When will it ever be

finished? we asked Richard. Two months, Richard guessed, maybe three. In the meantime, he suggested that rather than renewing the lease on the condo, we arrange to continue renting on a month to month basis, which would permit us to exit with two months' notice. Stay put, if you can, and be patient, he advised. He would tell us when it was safe to give notice.

That's what we did. We explained our situation to the condo rental people, who were very helpful. And we stayed on. And on. And on. As the end of 1994 drew nigh, we began thinking about the holidays. We wanted to be settled by then, so we could have our family Christmas Eve dinner with Lori and Ernie, and Brad, Jane, and their boys, Graeme and Matthew (our granddaughter Sarah hadn't been born yet). We also looked forward to a visit from that other wonderful wheaten terrier, Zoë. Plus, it was our turn to host New Year's Eve with our friends, Norma and Randall.

We got on Richard's case. We'd like to be in and settled before the year-end holidays, we told him. Would we make it? He wasn't sure. It was too soon to tell. There was still a lot to do. He'd let us know when it looked promising. We kept after him every month from then on. Finally, after several months of hearing "not yet," in August of 1994 Richard told us we should be able to move into the church loft in two months. The workmen

When the saints went marching out with the departing congregation, the lofters came marching in. Actually, we came walking in, but briskly.

The new entrance hall, through the saved double doors and high-lighted by the old church lamp.

The Urban Loft

A broader view of the stairs from the door level to the landing. The black square to the right is the door to our mailbox.

would still be there; they'd work around us. We could give notice. That would mean moving on October 30.

But somehow, after all our nagging, we were overcome with doubt. Just looking around, we found it difficult to believe that the church would be ready to accommodate us in two months. So we played it safe, waited another month, and then gave notice. That was it. We'd be moving on November 30. We booked a mover. We sent out change of address cards. And once again, we started to reduce what we deemed to be excess baggage: our surplus stuff, the expendables – not by selling them, I might add, but by giving them away to worthwhile groups that would have them, or, when that failed, to any unsuspecting individuals who mistook free for valuable.

As the two months drew to an end and our moving day drew ever closer, it became appallingly apparent that the half of the church over which we had jurisdiction was not yet ready to accept us into its chaotic embrace, dammit. After all we'd been through, we still wouldn't be able to move into the church at the end of November. Any job you'd care to mention was still incomplete. The place – I should call it the site, it was not yet a place – was still crawling with workmen and rife with dust and debris. The noise and the mess were beyond belief. As our moving day loomed, it became obvious that we'd have to camp elsewhere for a couple of weeks, and a nearby motel solved the problem. After consulting those coming between our space and us, we decided that our stuff, at least – our things, our goods, our chattels – could be moved into the loft, provided they were careful-

Under the real stairs, metal ravens stand on faux stairs that go nowhere but are handy to put stuff on and fun to answer questions about.

ly stacked and covered. Half a hallelujah!

As many of our possessions as possible would be jammed into the TV room/library on the main floor, rendering the room inaccessible to the workmen or us. The rest – the bulk, as it turned out – would be stacked in a large mound in the centre of the living room and covered with large blue tarpaulins to protect our value-baubles from John's crew of painters who were in attendance and who, in their white work wardrobe, would now have to dance around this blue knoll in a sort of tribal tribute to materialism.

To complicate matters, when the moving day arrived, the uncovered and restored maple floor was still wet in places from the oil and varnish treatment. The movers had to navigate across strategically placed planks before they could deposit our belongings – on more planks – on the newly varnished floor. You just can't win. At least, not without a lot of tarpaulins and planks.

The front entrance past the wooden handrail and through the perforated metal railing on the main level is different every time you look at it.

On moving day, as we relocated into a nearby motel and at the same time moved all our goods and chattels into the still-in-the-throes-of-conversion church, we were treated to a taste of our new neighbours' generous hospitality.

Neil and Sharon, the couple already resident in the rectory adjoining the church, had graciously extended an invitation to dinner. Possibly because they found that our renova-tion had about it a certain theatrical quality, they had prepared a huge ham to celebrate the occasion. It would be waiting, they told us. We were to come and dine with them whenever we were finished unloading and were free of the movers. We worried aloud that it could be late. No problem, we were assured. We were to come whenever we were through, no matter how late. We warned them that we had Satch, the wild wheaten, with us. No problem. We were to bring Satch. They loved dogs.

It took better than half the day to get everything out of the condo. And the rest of the day and well into the evening to unload it at the church. Mid-afternoon, between loads at the church, two ladies who lived in the house directly across the street from us appeared at our door. The mother, Linda, carried a silver tray with two cups of espresso on it, as well as biscotti, fruitcake, and linen napkins. Linda had little English, and the little she had was not all that intelligible to us and was interlaced with Italian, which was not at all intelligible to us. Her daughter, Louisa, therefore, translated both her mother's Italian and her English. The translated message was, in effect: Welcome. We're glad you're

Stairs from landing up to first level with Richard's beautifully detailed ziggurat of maple and steel which heightens the Hitchcockian entry effect.

here. Have a coffee and some cake. The sentiment was charming, the timing flawless.

The timing of dinner, however, was another matter. Unloading our possessions seemed to take forever. A larger moving truck could have handled the job in one load, but last minute mechanical problems had put it out of commission. The smaller truck that replaced it necessitated two loads and two trips. The job went slowly. Having to walk the planks and carefully stack everything so as to leave room for the workmen took longer than expected. It got later and later, darker and darker. By the time we were ready for dinner, it was 10:30 p.m.

Nonetheless, our hosts welcomed us with open arms – and I'm sure, raging appetites. The lord and lady of the rectory toasted us with wine in their living room. Satch tore around the unfamiliar surroundings, up and down the stairs, sniffing at everything in sight, while we worried that he might do something he'd enjoy and we'd regret. Our new friends told us not to worry. As part of the late evening's activities, Satch got up on their sofa and knocked off all the pillows. We later discovered that he had performed this trick on their bed as well. And when Richard arrived unexpectedly at Neil and Sharon's back door to ask us something before going home after a long day on the site, Satch performed his runaway brat trick, taking off through the open door and tearing down the lane with many people in dogged pursuit. We had to negotiate his return with treats. Cheese, if I remember correctly. Low-fat cheddar.

Later, close to midnight, I believe, as the ham was being put on the dining room table, Satch tried to clamber up and have a taste of the main course. Quick action by Colleen saved the day and the main course. This was new behaviour

These are the stair treads no one was permitted to tread on before the work was finished.

for the wild wheaten. Nor has he done it since. Maybe the straitjacket helped. Or the chains.

Satch was strongly chastised for his excessive interest. Deeply chagrined, he slunk away and hid in a dark corner. He was not heard from again until we were three-quarters of the way through our late, but lovely, candlelit dinner. At that point, all perky and waggy-tailed again, Satch reappeared to mooch scraps from his over-indulgent master and mistress and their friendly neighbours. Then, having wined and dined and talked for several hours, we made our weary way to our temporary digs at the nearby motor hotel, and our first night in between-homes limbo.

Colleen and I, along with Satch and our two ancient cars and our hand luggage, had found accommodation in a conveniently located, but not all that favourably reputed, motor hotel not too far from the church of our earnest intentions. (The hotel is the kind of place that makes people snicker when you tell them you're staying there.)

Fortunately, the motor hotel permitted canine pets and gave us a discounted weekly rate on a handy (for dog walking) ground-floor room. It also provided free parking for both our cars and free coffee in the lobby along with sugar doughnuts of uncertain provenance, though we did not avail ourselves of the latter two. The hotel desk staff, well acquainted with the reasons for our stay, were bemusedly helpful, though clearly they were not used to long staying guests. Most of their clientele were one-night stands. Or less. Twenty minutes was about average. But what the heck. That's life in the naked city.

Though decidedly unhappy that our plans had been messed up, we decided to make the best of it and treat our stay in the hotel as if it were a holiday, wandering around

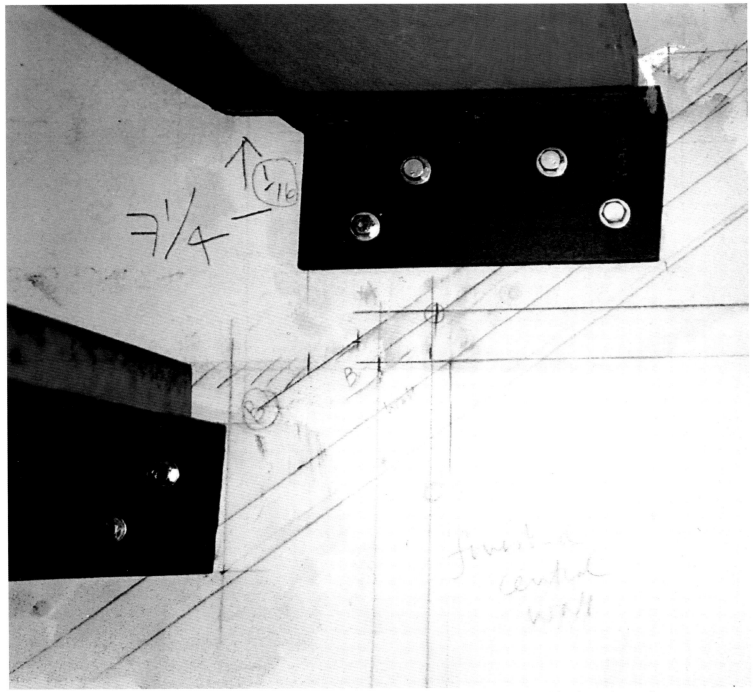

Angle irons cut from an old girder taken out of the roof when building the deck, now float the stairs. Note Richard's precise on-site measurements.

T h e U r b a n L o f t

Night view of our windows and their intriguing, yet not revealing, sightlines. Design of such excellence may threaten developers. I hope so.

the surrounding area, walking Satch in the nearby park, and trying out the neighbourhood restaurants. It was not an unpleasant experience. And because it was handy to the church, we could visit frequently to monitor progress, gauge the disaster level, or just get in the way of the workmen.

Finally, after two weeks of camping out in the confines of the colourful motor hotel, we were able to move bodily into what remained of the sanctity of the former church, reunited with our possessions just before the Christmas holiday. The work in the church, of course, was still far from over; and it went on around us daily. Hammers rang and saws buzzed; painters rolled and brushed; and workmen scurried all over the place.

It was bedlam.

And then, on the eve of Christmas, despite the disarray, we managed to have the whole family – children, grandchildren, and dogs (but not Lori and Ernie's two cats) – in for dinner, even though the kitchen still had no counter, no sink, no drain, no taps. We were able to prepare dinner, cook, and tidy up afterwards by washing dishes in the twelve-inch sink in the powder room.

We did it again on New Year's Eve, dining with friends Randall and Norma, and again relying on the sink in the powder room. We were so happy to be in our new home at last that none of the inconvenience seemed to matter.

In fact, for the first five months of that year, 1995, everything was extremely inconvenient. For five months, we lived with tradesmen. From early morning, they were there. From dawn to dusk and sometimes beyond, these assiduous and industrious agents of change were in our place, in our face, on our lap, at our tap, on our back, over our shoulder, by our side, at our elbow, overhead, underfoot. Wherever you looked, there they were, heads down, diligently working their butts off to finish our project so they could pack up, move on, and create chaos elsewhere for some other family.

Inevitably, we got to know the tradesmen; we made them coffee, served them cold drinks, bought them deadly doughnuts from the dismal doughnut shop about a block away. Colleen became so familiar to the doughnut mongers that they would have the doughnuts packaged up and ready as she came through the door. And, of course, our beverage bills went up.

And for two months, we were stairless. The easy way to the mezz would have been up Richard's beautiful floating maple staircase with treads that sat on small, metal brackets cut from the church's saved old steel trusses. The only problem was that the heavy solid maple stair treads custommade by a specialty woodworking shop were slow to arrive. When they did arrive, half of them were truly beautiful, and the other half were marred by marks from the planer and had to go back to be done again. I can't explain why they were delivered that way. They couldn't either.

And then, when we finally got all the treads back in proper shape, Richard wouldn't let Frank install them until all the dirty work in the loft was finished. Nothing was going to sully those beautiful treads before their time; not if Richard had his way. What about protective plywood covers? No. The treads would still get hacked up. Richard was adamant. Wait, he insisted. In the meantime, he told the workmen to use a ladder to get to the second floor. And they weren't the only ones who had to use the ladder. For those two months, when it came time to go to bed on our mezzanine, we ascended a ladder to get there. What's more, because it wasn't safe to leave Satch, the wild wheaten, alone downstairs amidst the upheaval of construction, we carried him, every night for two months, up the ladder to the mezzanine. Satch weighs forty-five pounds. We hadn't expected weightlifting to be part of our ordeal. But to be fair, I think I got my hernia from lifting something else. A horse, maybe. I know it wasn't the elephant I mentioned earlier.

At our request, the metal railings were designed by Richard to give a little industrial context to the space. A metalwork shop machined the metal components out of standard perforated sheet steel and square metal tubing. The shop edged the cut pieces of sheet steel with solid metal and then bent the sheets at right angles at both ends into kind of a rectangular u-shape. All the metal was sandblasted and powder treated to prevent oxidation. The treatment wasn't entirely successful. We were getting some oxidation, which interestingly gives the metal an aged look and is not unattractive.

The railings and the wooden handrails (handsomely fashioned by Frank) were simply assembled and installed with large nuts and bolts and washers, somewhat like a Meccano set. Colleen and I actually helped Richard assemble them.

To go with the maple of the restored original floor, we elected to use maple throughout not only for the handrails, stair treads, and wood trim but also for the sideboard in the dining room, the phone counter in the TV room, and the centre island in the kitchen, pairing it as often as we could with metal.

Once we were ensconced in the incompleteness of the loft, once we found ourselves living in a state of constant chaos, strange things began happening to our perceptions. Late one winter afternoon, for example, after the workmen had departed, the sawdust had settled, and the silence had descended on our residence-cum-building site, Colleen decided to walk out to the corner to get us some pizza for dinner.

It was snowing a little when Colleen went out. By the time she made her way back, determinedly clutching two pizza boxes, the snow had turned into a bit of a blizzard. As she passed Michael and Niamh's part of the church, she chanced to look up into one of their windows. Through the blowing snow, she saw a sight she couldn't believe. Inside our neighbours' loft was what appeared to be a magnificent staircase of steel and wood that ascended all the way to the roof. They had built a monumental staircase – our staircase, the delusionary staircase that Richard had talked us out of.

Colleen was astounded. How could this be? The pizza was getting cold. She put her head down again and mushed on. When she looked up again she realized that the window she had looked into wasn't Michael and Niamh's at all. It was our own. And what she had seen was not a staircase,

but the rented scaffolding, which we had lived with for months to permit the ever-present workmen to clamber to the top and wreak havoc in high places.

We actually grew quite fond of the scaffolding, even jokingly discussing the possibility of retaining it as a permanent installation, a kind of giant sculpture. (Or better yet, maybe we could get a nice, new, shiny one.) Ultimately, good sense prevailed; the scaffolding was torn asunder and went back to the rental depot whence it came. Great shame, in a way. It would have been impressive in our living room. Not too many living rooms have them. And it would have made wall cleaning and window washing so much easier. (And dusting the ceiling; let's not forget dusting the ceiling.)

In the disorderly buzz all around us, all sorts of oddball notions that had never occurred to us before began popping up. For example, as we looked bemusedly about us one day, we realized suddenly, as if in an epiphany, that with Michael and Niamh's home on one side of us and Neil and Sharon's on the other side, our abode – despite its scale, despite its vast volume – was, in fact, really nothing more than the centre row house in a row of three. What's more, it was the only one of the three that, in keeping with the minimalist intentions of its possibly delusionary but certainly determined owners, had only one bedroom. Good God, we were living in what some future real estate ad might quite accurately describe as:

One-bedroom row house, 1-1/2 bathrooms, partially finished basement, high ceilings, quiet, downtown neighbourhood.

And then one day, the din stopped, the dust disappeared and the tradesmen left and did not return. The work was done. The loft was ours and ours alone.

But not for long.

COCK-A-DOODLE-DOO!

Early one morning, shortly after we moved into the church, Colleen was awakened by the crowing of a rooster. Had I heard the rooster crowing in the middle of the night? she wondered over our supplement-enhanced, high-fibre, low-fat, cholesterol-free breakfast.

"A rooster?" I responded in disbelief, nearly spilling the skim milk cappuccino that I was raising to my mouth. No, I hadn't heard any rooster. Churches don't have roosters. Churches have angels. And I hadn't heard any of those either.

It happened again the next day. The rooster crowed in the early morning darkness, once again waking you know who. I heard nothing. The crowing of the rooster, Colleen advised me at breakfast the next day, appeared to be coming from the direction of the back lane.

I insisted that there were no roosters in downtown Toronto. But Colleen was certain that a little inner-city poultry farming was what we're dealing with and returned her attention to her oatmeal and multi-grain toast.

Driven by curiosity, we asked around and, sure enough, our investigations led us to a nearby city-centre chicken farm. Right behind it, under the same astute management, was an urban rabbit ranch. There it was. Just across the lane and slightly south of us, a neighbour kept chickens and rabbits in pens of his own construction, cleverly recycling their waste as fertilizer. The friendly retired contractor had – on a small scale – returned to his early Portuguese farm roots in the Azores. He invited us in for a tour.

He had owned a small two-storey house on the lane. When the house next to it came up for sale, he bought it,

acquiring ownership of two side-by-side houses. He and his wife lived in one and rented out the other. He "farmed" the adjoining yards in both. In addition to chickens and rabbits, he grew bountiful crops of sweet corn and tomatoes and lettuce and broccoli and various other greens and grapes, all of which he generously handed out to neighbours, us among them, to sample.

Our mini-farmer is just one of the interesting things about our lane. Narrow as streets go, but wide as lanes go, our saintly lane, unlike most back lanes, is clean. What's more, the garages on this handy little passageway are all relatively new and in good repair.

Just north on the lane is another interesting phenomenon: a row of lane houses. These little homes – there are five of them – are conversions of old carriage houses, stables, or garages behind full-sized houses. Some are single storey, some multi-storey. Some even have basements dug out. All of them have street numbers, and mail is delivered right to the door. Starter homes for younger couples, most of whom are childless, these places appear to be nicely finished. We visited one that had at one time been lived in by a young carpenter and his wife. He had done the wee place over in all sorts of interesting woods. After he and his wife had a child, they moved away, selling their home to a retired fellow, who got himself a charming little spot from which he cycles vigorously around the area.

Except for the postal carrier, few people know that these secret houses are there with real people living in them: tiny hideaways in a back lane with a saint's name, where early every morning a rooster crows to awaken the day.

CHAPTER 14

REACHING FOR THE SUN

The two big windows in the living room face north, letting cool north light (painter's light, some call it) into the building. Only briefly, late in the day – and only at certain times of the year – does any direct sunlight come through these windows.

Richard, our indispensable architectural mentor and guide, had suggested early on that getting a little more direct sunlight – a few precious, golden rays from the south – into the living room would be helpful aesthetically, as it would brighten up the space in varying but always interesting ways at different times of the year. He proposed to accomplish this with a sort of clerestory on the south side of the living-room wall which, along with an upper deck with stairs leading to it, had been in the original design. But now we were so worn out by having

the workmen constantly around, and also concerned about the cost that we decided to delay any work on the upper level until we were in better shape, in every sense. Whereupon, we had kicked the workmen out of our castle, filled the moat with sharks, hauled up the drawbridge, and held off for a couple of months before deciding to let them back in to finish Richard's plan.

Having explained the hiatus that preceded the building of the clerestory, let me also explain the clerestory itself. But first, a message from the past. The traditional clerestory of classical architecture was usually a raised construction with windows in it, which sat on the roof of a building. Rising above the surrounding rooftops, the clerestory let light into the interior of the building on which it sat. Our modified version of the clerestory – the one we finally agreed to – does not rise up from the roof but, in effect, descends from it. This cleverly conceived natural light source is a large, vertical glass-block window at the top of the south wall of our living room. Designed as three side-by-side panels, twenty-three blocks wide by seven blocks deep, it gives us a window – one hundred and sixty-one glass blocks in all – right at ceiling level. At right angles to this window, at the top of the west wall in our bedroom, is a fourth panel of forty-nine glass blocks. This lets some southwest light into the bedroom, from which a little also spills into the living room.

When these glass-block windows were first installed earlier in the renovation, the other side

Roof deck being built. It was, in effect, a room with the roof torn off, a room in the sky.

Roof deck in full bloom. The plants love it up here. It's so bright in the summer that we had to put up an awning.

The Urban Loft

Through the trees, past the periwinkle to one of the basement windows. In the right kind of weather, we are an oh-so-green establishment.

steel I-beams that, painted bright red to match the bright red door, give the deck an imaginary roof line and provide an anchoring place for the large awning that we improvised from a bright blue construction tarpaulin and four bungee cords.

Notable among the features in this roofless room in the sky are wall panels of gleaming corrugated steel siding that rise to the edge of the cutaway roof and are highlighted by black metal flashing. Above the waterproof, black rubber under-deck, a raised and removable over-deck of wooden pallets was installed and stained gray. A water tap was put into the wall, not only to lend some point to the floor drain but also to facilitate our rooftop gardening efforts, which include a very beautiful Japanese red maple in a huge wooden barrel.

There are also a number of flowers and plants in another wooden barrel, and a few tomato plants and a park bench that Colleen painted bright yellow. And, for dining in the sky, we found a small, round, lime-green patio table and four comfortable black mesh chairs. In the right weather, it is heaven on high.

of the glass was still dark attic space beneath the church roof. To get outside light to the clerestory windows, Richard planned a cutout in the roof, which would expose three interior vertical surfaces and a horizontal surface. This space – a roof deck, essentially – would give us a convenient place to loll about doing irreparable sun damage to our skin.

When Richard first suggested this roof deck, Colleen saw its possibilities immediately. I had to be persuaded. And I'm pleased that I was. The result is spectacular. Picture, if you will, a room with the ceiling removed, a room in the sky, a high-level hideaway, isolated from everything around it, totally private, and flooded with sunlight most of the year. When we don't get in its way, the sunlight streams through the clerestory into our living room.

When the roof was punched out, some of the steel strutwork had to be cut away. But we retained three overhead

After the construction of the clerestory, the building of the deck, and the extending of our stairs up to deck level, we added to the top of the church next to the deck a little room with an ensuite bathroom. From that room, three windows look out on the deck. Before we knew it, right under the roof, we had the beginnings of a third floor, one we hadn't

The ground floor deck, a small pretty space between buildings. It's long and narrow and a great place to send indoor plants to summer camp.

The Urban Loft

Our discreet yet intriguing front entrance today. If you didn't know better, you'd think someone important lived here. But it's just us.

planned on and that I have no intentions of finishing. Are you listening, Richard? Are you listening Colleen? No intentions.

I've never pretended to expertise with plants, yet I've always had a great fondness for them. We've always had a few palms around – bamboos, areatas, marginatas. We have a five-foot kentia palm, for example, which we bought almost twenty years ago for a darkish corner in the old Vic, specifically because we were told that kentias thrive in low light. This tree has, in fact, thrived in almost no light at all and is still around to this day. Though it hasn't grown much, it's still in good shape.

We have also had philodendrons of different kinds, though not always for long. But one split leaf – salloum by name – has been with us for twenty-five years. No matter how much abuse it took from being moved, from accidents, from unintentional neglect, it always came back bigger, stronger, greener. Today, it's a giant green octopus in a large and extremely heavy pot. It takes a dolly (the kind with wheels) and two people – ideally, in trusses – to move it.

The graceful *Ficus benjamina,* the weeping fig, was always a great favourite of ours. We grew some modest ficuses into fair-sized trees. But they were always very sensitive to change: light, heat, humidity, placement, whatever. Moving as often as we did was hard on them. They disliked disruption of any kind. (You couldn't even curse in their presence!) If things didn't suit them, in a flash they'd drop all their leaves.

I had often said to Colleen that if we ever got a loft with a ceiling high enough, it might provide us an opportunity to put in a big ficus. Now that we had the space, all we had to do was find a big ficus. But first, we had to find a plant dealer who dealt in big trees. Few do, we discovered. Finally, we located an excellent greenhouse out in the northeastern 'burbs.

We explained our quest for a large ficus to the proprietor and described the space and light in the renovated church. He had many big ficuses but was strongly opposed to selling one to us. These plants needed more southern light, he

Another view of the front with the awning above and the trellis on the right. The tree in front is a honey locust.

said, and wouldn't thrive in the mostly northern light of our latter-day palazzo. Our best bet, he advised, was a kentia palm. We would have liked a kentia about twenty feet tall. But the biggest kentias available at the time were twelve footers. In order to make a statement, we bought four of them. I'm not sure exactly what that statement was. All I know is that it was green. It still is.

In addition to the trees inside, we have quite a few trees in our front yard along the side of the building. I should explain that the entire church building extended to the lot line on the east and on the north. Like many of the front yards in this area, ours (which was the former church's side yard) was actually on city property, which we are permitted to use and for which we are expected to care. And we do. We care a great deal for this outer extension to our premises. Right from the beginning, we did quite a bit to beautify it, much to the benefit of both the building and the street.

On what had been a small fenced side lawn, which ran the length of the building, we installed, in concert with our next-door neighbours to the east, a line of tall Siberian crab apple trees. Six of these lofty beauties are on our part of the property, to the east of our front door. They set off our windows, giving the illusion of privacy without being at all hedge-like. These trees are columnar. They don't spread their limbs. Instead, they grow their branches straight up. Interestingly and oddly, the trees are sterile, flowering early and bearing tiny green crab apples, fruit the size of peas, which turn yellow in the autumn but do not fall, remaining on the trees after the leaves drop, to be eaten during the winter by the hungry sparrows, starlings, and chickadees.

The Siberian crab apple trees being planted. They've grown a lot since then. According to Siberian authorities, they can grow to forty feet.

Just west of our front door, in a little patch of small pebbles against our other neighbour's fence, we planted a lovely, lacy honey locust that has grown up to our second floor and now just peeks above my office window.

Perhaps I should explain about the pebbles. Ours is a graceful but grassless front yard. We decided early on that we had cut enough grass in our lives and didn't want to do it anymore. (No mow.) Upon making this decision, we bestowed our power mower on a delighted friend. In lieu of grass, on the street edge of the yard, Terry, the landscaper who had put in the trees, designed a good-looking and easy-to-care-for configuration of ground cover around the

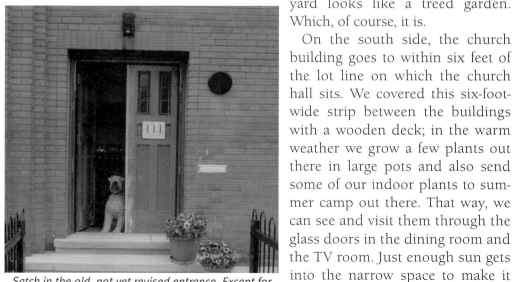

Satch in the old, not yet revised entrance. Except for the postie, Satch felt that anyone coming to our door was coming to see him.

trees. It was mostly periwinkle and a little ajuga with a scalloped border of small pebbles in the middle of the yard. Square flagstones finished off the garden to the building wall. Three Boston ivy plants were planted against the pilasters in the wall and slowly but relentlessly have made their way skyward up the columns. Amidst all this was an array of pots of various sizes containing a variety of colourful blooming plants. Inside the old wrought-iron fence, which was rejigged slightly to make the whole thing work, the front yard looks like a treed garden. Which, of course, it is.

On the south side, the church building goes to within six feet of the lot line on which the church hall sits. We covered this six-foot-wide strip between the buildings with a wooden deck; in the warm weather we grow a few plants out there in large pots and also send some of our indoor plants to summer camp out there. That way, we can see and visit them through the glass doors in the dining room and the TV room. Just enough sun gets into the narrow space to make it look like a hot house, which, unfortunately, it isn't.

CHAPTER 15

TOUCHING FINISHES

Towards the end of the construction process, when work was being done in the attic area of the church, we discovered that our one-bedroom row house had a leak in its sloped roof. But winter was approaching, and the sloped roof was icy and, if accessible, probably risky for the accessors. Repairs would have to wait till weather permitted. Fortunately, the roofer assured us, the leak was minor. Not to worry. It would necessitate only a small repair job in the spring; a few shingles would need to be removed, replaced, or added, and the problem would go away. We would be high and dry. Or dry on high.

In the meantime, at Richard's suggestion, to keep water from getting into the renovated part of the building (and dampening our living space as well as our spirits), we hung a large tarpaulin hammock-like under the leak to catch the water coming in. It did this admirably all winter.

In the spring, when the roofers clambered up onto the roof, they found that the leaking area already had three layers of shingles on it, which, it was explained to us, was at least one layer too many. Apparently the roof had leaked in the past and been shingled over twice before. Adding another layer of shingles would not solve the problem. To correct the leak, all the shingles in that area of the roof had to come off, and shingling had to start all over again. This, we were depressed to learn, meant replacing half the roof. Half-heartedly we did so. It was more overhead, overhead.

While we never hung window coverings, we did hang a lot of other stuff: banners, paintings, light sculptures. Having settled in without drapes, their absence never troubled us. The sightlines from the street are such that people walking by see in only in a partial and very fragmented way. They see the ceiling and high up on the concrete-block wall, they see thirteen intricate and colourful banners that Colleen designed years ago (page 39). They are based on the thirteen-stanza poem, "Thirteen Ways of Looking at a Blackbird," by the American poet Wallace Stevens, whose poetry Colleen had studied and loved at school in Baltimore. For several years, while I was in

The multi-drawer chest left behind in the sacristy once held priestly vestments. Moved down to Colleen's studio by four workmen, it now holds artwork.

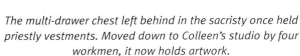

Entrance hall steel and plywood, boot removers' bench designed by Colleen. Heads above by sculptor Libby Faux.
Red alarm on left by fire department.

business, the banners dominated the lobby, always receiving positive comments from visitors, not only for the subtlety of design but also for the unusual combinations of fabrics – cottons and linens and wools and silks and sari cloth with gold thread – that had gone into their creation. And also for the dazzling juxtapositions of colour: sombre black and white, and striking red and sunny orange and, in one instance, verdant green.

Richard had never seen the banners. When we showed them to him and told him we hoped to hang them high on the block wall, he reacted with enthusiasm, offering to help devise a method of fastening them to the concrete. He came up with a simple and elegant idea. He cut a bunch of little hardwood strips, which could be easily hammered into the mortar lines in the wall. Into these bits of wood, stickpins could be pushed, from which the banners would hang. The wood strips would be hidden so the banners would appear to float. Magic. That's what people walking by see through our windows, floating banners against a block wall.

They also see the aforementioned south-facing glass-block clerestory, a sort of skylight out to the roof deck. And they see the tops of our indoor trees. But rarely, even though we are there, do they see us lurking on the other side of the glass. They do see Satch, our good-lurking wheaten terrier, of course, because he likes to lie on the window seat with his nose to the glass as he surveys the street.

On a couple of occasions, when I've been out inspecting the periwinkle in the front garden, a passerby has stopped, peered upwards into our windows (they're nine feet above street level), looked at the banners, looked at the plants, and then turned to me in puzzlement.

"Excuse me," the person has said, pointing to our windows. "But is that the lobby to the condos next door?"

"Yes, it is," I've learned to respond, as if I were the condo superintendent. To explain that it wasn't the lobby but was the unlikely living room of a private residence almost always leads me into a lengthy monologue about renovation and conversion, which I'd decided, after the first few of these impromptu briefing sessions, to save for this book.

Did I mention that the entrance floor is covered with charcoal-coloured bargain tiles that we stumbled on? (Fortunately, no one has stumbled on them since.) They look and feel like stone. We're not sure what they're actually made of. They could be concrete, or very old cheddar. They're very, very serviceable. The amazing thing is they only cost a dollar each. They may be the only bargain in the whole place, except maybe for the eight-dollar tarpaulin doubling as a sunshade up on the roof deck.

Everyone says that the bench sitting on the tiles in the front hall looks like it's always been there. But it's not an original church artifact. We thought it would be handy to have a bench at the door, especially in the winter so people could sit and take off their boots. Colleen drew a little sketch, and a craft shop made it up out of laser-cut maple plywood fastened to square metal tubing. The cutout in the plywood back of the bench repeats the grid design of the windows and the block wall and the metal in the bench picks up the metal in the railings on the various landings.

The four large drawings of tools on the entry hall walls were rendered in graphite on brown kraft paper by Colleen. The wrench and the two types of pliers were inspired by all the workmen's tools around for months during the renovation. The winged corkscrew, of course, was based on one of our kitchen tools. It was the device of choice in moments of high angst.

From the front hall, stairs lead down to the basement. I guess, in retrospect, that we treated these stairs as service stairs. They're tucked out of sight and don't have floating maple treads. (Mind you, the handrail on the wall is maple.) They're functional stairs and get us down to and up from the basement.

The thing that's significant about the basement is that it's mostly above grade. As a result, the windows are above the ground and let in lots of light.

Like the big windows in the living room, the studio windows let northern light into the studio. For security, because they're close to grade level, we put hinged wooden doors over the windows that can be let down and locked

Studio in basement, well lit by above-ground windows.

down into the studio where Colleen now uses it to store drawings and paintings and paper. It's been very handy. The original hand-lettered labels in fading ink from church days are still on the drawer fronts. A visiting parishioner who came to see what we'd done with his old praying ground spotted the labels. "I made those labels," he said, not without a catch in his voice.

In the garage we added hot and cold water taps and a drain that makes it handy for washing the car (we have only one now), which we rarely (i.e., never) do. We're afraid to. It's an old car. The dirt is all that holds it together. The taps are handy for washing Satch's feet when he comes in muddy from the park, which is often.

Behind a little blue door in the corner of the basement that you have to stoop to get through there's one more tiny room under the cellar stairs, a sort of sub-basement, an old, low-ceilinged, left-over space that could have been made (and might still be, I suppose) into a bathroom, or sauna, or wine cellar, or phone booth. It has a little landing in it and a few decaying stairs down to ancient, cracked concrete. We opted to leave this little nook the way we found it. It's what the place looked like before the renovation. We put a light in it, store a few things in it, but otherwise have left it the way it was as kind of a memorial to the way it was. We call it "the bilge."

From the basement up to roof deck, it's forty-seven steps, broken by landings and returns into seven flights. The biggest, at the bottom, has eleven steps. The very smallest, at the top, has only one step. And in between, there's a nine, three sevens, and a five. I recite this

from inside. Mostly, the doors are pulled up on pulleys and kept flush with the ceiling.

Inside the studio, to the left of the door is another saved church artifact, a big wide cabinet – of oak – with large, wide, shallow drawers that were once used to store priestly vestments. The cabinet was left behind in what was the sacristy (and is now the TV room) probably because it was very heavy and difficult to move. With the help of a bunch of tradesmen – the strong ones – we managed to wrestle it because the stairs are my health club. Going up and down all day gives me a good workout.

Once you've huffed your way up to the landing on the roof deck level, you look over the railing and down into the living room and it's like looking down from the top deck of an ocean liner. (I'm guessing. I've never been on an ocean liner.)

There's a little sitting room up there with a window looking out on the deck. Two inflatable clear plastic chairs, a little plaster pillar table with a lamp with a blue shade on it, a little round glass table with a cordless phone on it, a few cushions, a few books, half a dozen small paintings on two of the walls. A hideout, a quiet place, right under the roof, to sit, to read, to think. A good concept. But it's theoretical. We almost never use it. It could be a guest bedroom, but we'd have to buy a bed.

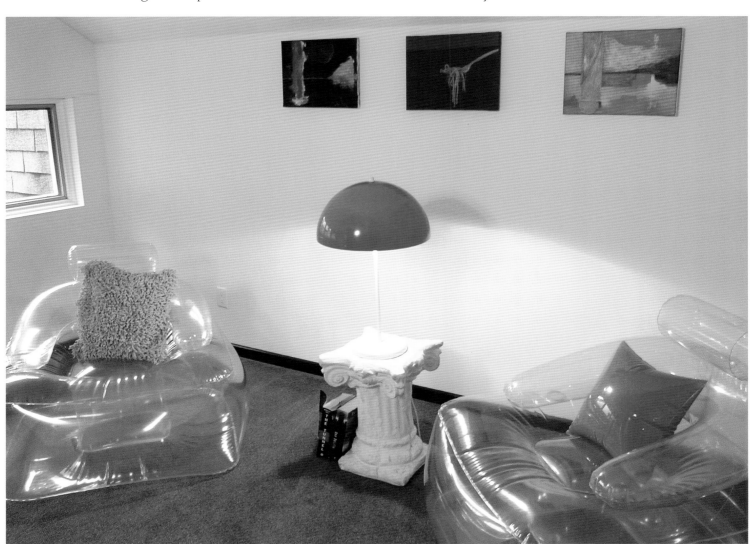

The lovely, quiet top-floor sitting room in which we never sit. It could be a bedroom but we have no bed.

CHAPTER 16

AN INSIDE VIEW

Well, now that the work is finished (it never is in a loft, and especially with these particular owners, but please bear with me), let me take you on a tour of this unusual space of ours. Let's start with the living room.

This room, obviously, is what this place is all about. It's the biggest, loftiest space in the whole structure and the centrepiece of the renovation. With the interior so open, the living room becomes the town square. It's at the heart of everything going on here. And the openness is enhanced by the light coming in the large windows. The look of the room – your view of it – is constantly changing as the light changes or as you move around it. But no matter what, it's always breathtaking.

This is probably a good place to talk about the colour palette of our space. Taking our cue from the natural materials used in the construction – the maple floor, the concrete block wall, the glass windows, the glass block – we chose to use natural elements wherever possible and keep the basic palette neutral. The inside window frames, for example, maintained their natural aluminum silver-gray colour. The stair railings stayed their natural steel-gray colour. The saved aluminum and glass church lamps stayed their natural colour. And the white drywall was painted even whiter with gallery white.

Where in this neutral palette was colour to come from? From paintings on the walls, from furniture on the floor, and from paint on the doors. Colleen painted all the inside doors with five coats of brilliant red, green, marigold, or blue enamel to add bright columns of colour to our decor.

Set against that mostly neutral background, the few ancient pieces of living room furniture that we've hung onto (clung grimly to, might be more appropriate) continue the colour contrast. This is especially true of the two wonderful time-worn but timeless red spandrel chairs, a design based on bridge spans. You'd never know it but the chair frames are plywood meticulously cut and glued and joined and then painstakingly sanded and buffed and then sprayed with maybe ten coats of bright red lacquer that are now starting to wear away in high traffic areas like the arms. The chairs are very comfortable. The angle of the arms and the rake of the back are exactly right, somehow, and sitting is softened by two black leather cushions filled with

Frank and Richard on the roof deck. Work must have been going well, they're both smiling. Or maybe it was being out in the sunlight.

The centrepiece of our renovation, the lofty living room, suddenly revealed upon climbing the stairs.

The Urban Loft

Looking west from living room: floating stairs, raven perched above, hanging painting and glassblock window.
Could be a book cover. As a matter of fact ...

T h e   U r b a n   L o f t

dense foam rubber, one of which lies on the seat bottom (on rubber webbing) while the other leans against the solid back.

The biggest pieces of furniture here are the two much scratched (i.e., much Satched) white leather sofas. We bought them about twenty-five years ago to fit the living room in the old Vic, a much more limited space. We'd like new sofas. But because these have stood up well to decades of depredation by dog claws, we're unlikely to replace them soon. We tell ourselves distressed leather works, at least around here.

There are also two hacked-up black, melamine-covered, particle-board coffee tables that our grandchildren play games on and under, as well as three handy little nesting tables of black metal with industrial style safety-glass tops, plus another of the saved church lamps, unchained, up-ended, and reincarnated as a fourth side table. Instead of spreading out all over the room, we've bunched all the furniture into a compact sitting and talking arrangement around a funky black and tan carpet, which Colleen set at a designedly askew angle in the middle of our huge space. The carpet has all kinds of furniture designs whimsically woven into it. The grand piano is my personal favorite. (I'm actually thinking of taking carpet lessons.)

Around this small conversational island set in a sea of maple flooring, we have strategically plant-

The dining room as seen from the living room. Everything in this place can be seen from almost everywhere else except from the underground garage.

ed three halogen lamps – two floor lamps and a table lamp – and our four kentia palms. It's funny about the dark green colour of the kentias. It not only fits in comfortably with all the natural/neutral tones but it also bridges between those neutrals and the bright colours.

There are four light sculptures. In the corner to the left of the windows and lit by four halogen spotlights is an installation-cum-sculpture called *Holding Cells*. It's made of wire mesh, cast plaster, and plywood. The other sculptures, all lit incandescently from within, include, on the wall unit, a large, green translucent pear, and on the walls at the back, two giant insects, one red, one yellow, crafted from plastic packaging fastened to wire legs made from coat hangers.

Between the windows, and fashioned in maple with shelf extenders of metal, is our Drdla-designed ziggurat-shaped wall unit, which serves as our stereo centre, CD repository, and recent book bunker. And, under the maple window seats flanking the shelving, the perforated steel of the stair

Richard's ziggurat bookcase with our sound system and the glowing electric pear on the outside wall of the living room between the big windows.

railings is repeated as a design element.

All the lesser rooms on the main floor have normal ceiling heights because they're under the L-shaped mezzanine overlooking the living room. Our concrete block wall continues into the dining room where the long maple sideboard attached to it does away with the need for a buffet. It's not only handy for serving buffet style (which we try not to do; we like to eat sitting down) but also for putting flowers on, for resting paintings on, or just to look at. This handsome sideboard sits on concrete blocks intentionally left protruding from the wall when it was built, fastened to them by two steel plates.

Our white Parson's dining table is another of our ancient artifacts. It's long and narrow because it was made originally for the narrow dining space in the sunroom of the old Vic. The table with four insertable leaves extends to seat twelve people comfortably. A round or square table would better suit our eighteen-foot-square dining space, but rectangular is what we have.

The dining room chairs are fairly recent. We bought them after moving into the church. The spare, open Italian design appealed to us. We liked the red metal frames contrasting with the black leather-like supporting surfaces.

The two double-glazed doors with the four handles – they look like supermarket freezer doors – on the south wall of the dining room are meant to be windows, but they're big enough to let us step out onto the long narrow deck space between our place and the church hall.

Under a painting of five golden sheep grazing unconcernedly on a cliff edge is the pass-through from the dining room into the kitchen, designed to keep the kitchen in touch with the dining room and also to double as a little bar for snacking while seated on the three black bar stools under it.

On the other side of the kitchen and tucked in beside the stairs, past a coat closet jammed with coats, is a compact powder room with its red door, green rubber tile floor, and a little round stainless steel sink. It's somewhat like an airplane washroom but less cramped.

The library-cum-TV room was originally planned as Colleen's office. But when Colleen started painting, she found it made better sense to combine her office with her studio in the basement. So the TV and VCR got moved into this room with most of our books. The room is sort of a jumble and a bit on the dark side. Fortunately, it gets a little light through the glass door that

Now, the photographers are even climbing on computer gear. This view of my office bookcase is from my laser printer.

leads out to the narrow deck between us and the church hall, and also from the window on the west wall that looks out over rectory neighbours Neil and Sharon's garage roof. The room also has a built-in maple counter on which our cordless phone/digital answering machine sits, making weird, distorted recordings of telephone messages, despite its vaunted digital acuity.

After the stairs to the mezzanine finally went in, I'd find myself standing on the second-floor landing overlooking the living room, and I'd be tempted to give guests below a

regal wave. The floor on the landing is not maple. We thought it might be fun to introduce another natural material compatible in colour and texture with our maple and metal choices. So we covered the landing with cork tile, which extends into my office and gives me a nice relaxed ambience to work in, and an earth-toned floor to roll around on in the ergonomic swivel chair that I spend much of my day in since I labour in our loft.

One of the other interesting features of my office – besides its occupant, I like to think – is the commanding

The overladen desk, one way of looking at my workspace. I reduce the paper buildup religiously. Clearly, more religion is needed.

desks; two comfortable swivel chairs; and wires, wires, many wires leading to all the digital gear I'll talk about in a moment, plus piles of paper waiting to be filed or tossed or shuffled, or just waiting to be waiting. Despite my pretensions to minimalism, I'm guilty of writer's clutter. I'm a data collector. The clippings and references seem to pile up. I throw paper out daily, religiously recycling it, but clearly more religion is required.

Like many writers, I've spent most of my life communicating. Or trying to. And to facilitate my doing so, I've assembled, in my office, in my car, on my person, many devious digital technological communications devices: a computer and monitor; a laser printer; a colour printer; a scanner; a fax machine-plus-copier; a two-line, cordless phone; a cell phone.

Despite all these high-tech toys, for some reason, old low-tech mail, snail mail as it's now called, still matters greatly (i.e., unreasonably) in my scheme of things. We get a great deal of mail. I watch for it. I wait for it. I fret over it. I like to open it before making any decisions about my day's activities. I'm sure that in some arcane compendium of infirmities there's a name for this one. I don't know what it is. I probably wouldn't like it, if I found out.

My office, of course, is where I deal with the mail – that is, if we're fortunate enough to receive it. If I may be permitted a brief digression, from the moment we moved in, we had problems with our mail. Our street number was the same as Neil and Sharon's next door in the rectory, except that our number was followed by the letter "A," which was followed by confusion. They got our mail. We got their mail. Once in a while, we got half theirs, half ours, and they got half ours, half theirs. It drove me half-nuts, half-sane.

view of the main-floor living area. On the short arm of the L-shaped mezzanine and open to the interior of the building, my workplace is, in effect, an office on a balcony; a room with an inner view. North light comes in through a lovely window, a baby brother of the big fellows in the living room. My office window matches the big guys in design and in width, though it's shorter in height. Like them, it looks out onto the street.

All the standard office stuff is present: a wall of bookcases; a filing cabinet (with filing cabinet magnets on it); two

Deciding we needed a new, less confusing street number, I asked my sister and brother-in-law Fran and Ken, lawyers both, to apply to the city to use a new, carefully researched, properly sequenced street number. For a fee, the city made the requested number street legal. In a moment of ingenious generosity, my counsellors paid the fee themselves, didn't charge for their efforts, and presented the new street number to us as a housewarming gift. I know of no one who has ever received a housewarming gift as sensible as a new house number. A street number never gets put into storage. It's always out there for all to see and admire. And best of all, once we had our own freestanding street number, the old mail confusion went away.

It was, unfortunately, quickly replaced by new mail confusion. I had promptly informed the post office of our new number and sent out changes of address all over again to absolutely everyone, including people I'd never heard of and who had never heard of me. Despite this, our usually substantial volume of mail diminished to a trickle and then dried up totally.

Then, I got a call from a guy twelve miles away in Scarborough. He had tracked me down to let me know he had all my mail, weeks of it, piles of it, bags of it. He had hesitated to put it back into the unreliable system that had carelessly sent it all to him. I went and gratefully collected my mail.

Looking into why we were suffering from mal de mail, I discovered, in *Perly's Toronto and Area Map Book,* that there were nine streets with the same name as ours. It was idiotic. You'd think there'd be enough names to go around.

To cap it off, one day I got a card from a newsletter publisher telling me they had been informed by U.S. Post (which I presume had been so advised by Canada Post) that my address did not exist. Strangely, the card telling me this had been correctly delivered to my "non-existent" address.

If you ever have mail problems, fax or e-mail your complaint to the postal authorities. That way, you'll know they'll get it. But whatever you do, don't bother changing your street number. It won't help.

Third-floor bathroom seen from the hallway. It was supposed to be a guest bathroom. But our guests don't want to stay in the bathroom.

Digression over. Back to the rest of the mezz level which isn't floored with maple either. It's carpeted, except for the bathroom and the laundry room, in dark, smoky-green wool sisal. This includes the mezzanine hallway, with halogen footlights near the floor, which goes past the dressing room on the right and continues into the bedroom. The large window cutout across from the dressing room and the three other window cutouts in the bedroom, all with three-foot-deep tiled ledges, all overlook the living room.

Under the wall cutouts in the hall are four storage cabinets – I keep office supplies in two of them. Under the cutouts in the bedroom there are also shelves for books and for my workout equipment. In addition, across from the

Oval washbasin in main-floor powder room. The sheep here for the annual zoo convention mistook the washbasin for a watering hole.

unexpected – and perhaps overly cautious – floor drain (a memorial to a long-ago flooding in another home).

Next to the laundry room, and behind a marigold door, the main bathroom is spacious to a fault. It would be easy, of course, to lay blame for this fault on my memories of the busy bathroom of my childhood, or on my recollections of the highly constricted, all-purpose bathroom of our mobile home days. But if you will permit me to go further afield in an attempt at justification, I could lay blame on yet another bathroom in a room we stayed in at the Fielding Hotel in London, once the home of eighteenth-century novelist, playwright, and journalist Henry Fielding.

So small was our room at the Fielding, so almost wall-to-wall with bed, that you had to sidle between the bed and the wall just to enter the room. Alternatively, you could, upon entering the room, throw yourself onto the bed and roll vigorously to your destination. Which brings us to the bathroom.

With two people in the room, if one of them wanted to enter the bathroom, the other had to go out into the hallway to permit opening of the bathroom door. Tiny and tubless, the bathroom had a shower compartment that was so confined, if you dropped the soap, you could not bend over to pick it up.

The method we developed to deal with this dilemma (now taught as The Fielding Technique) was as follows: Turn shower off. Open shower door. Step out of shower stall. Keeping door open, bend over. Reach back into shower stall and carefully pick up soap. Clutching soap firmly, straighten up. Step back into shower stall. Close door. Turn shower on. Repeat as necessary.

dressing room, one on each side of the big cutout, are two closets, with blue folding doors behind which we store mostly off-season stuff.

Off the mezz hall, and close to where most laundry originates, behind a red door is the laundry room. If cleanliness is next to godliness, this is the most important room in the house. The laundry room has all the things in it you'd expect, washer, dryer, ironing board, iron, sink, work counter, storage shelving, washing supplies. It's pretty basic, except for three things. One is its brilliant (i.e., sensible) location on the second floor. Since space permitted, it made sense not to lug the laundry down two flights to the basement to wash it, and then lug it back up again. Two is its attractive floor covering of blue rubber. And three is its

Something about the bathroom makes people smile. Maybe it's the colour combination in the tiles or maybe it's because they don't have plumbing.

Or I could lay blame on another small bathroom in a cramped hotel room we stayed in at the Shoreham in New York. Upgrading the old hotel, with gleaming appointments, fine art, and interesting furniture had not increased the size of the rooms, at least not the one we stayed in. In the miniature bathroom, it was almost impossible to towel yourself off after a shower because the bath towel was longer than the room was wide. So narrow was the bath-room that to get around, you had to inch between the exquisite wash basin and the regal toilet bowl. When you managed – only by straddling – to descend to the throne, your knees went under the wash basin, putting the basin, in effect, in your lap. This was a somewhat pinched arrangement, but it made possible the performance of all your ablutions in one sitting, if you were so inclined.

But enough of this tight-toilet trauma and back to our

The shower stall by who remembers? Towel art by N.Y. street artist Keith Haring.

own bathroom. Despite a small frosted-glass window that doesn't let in much light, the bathroom is always bright and sunny thanks to Richard's carefully designed arrangement of colourful wall tiles: navy blue and white and gray and sunny marigold tiles joyously juxtaposed and set off by gleaming black rubber on the floor.

Plumbing and hardware are good quality but not particularly splashy. Though we rarely use it, except to bathe Satch, we also put in a good-sized but otherwise undistinguished soaker tub. We had discussed, but resisted, installing a whirlpool tub. We had one in the condo but rarely found time to use it and didn't much care for it when we did. (Neither did Satch. In fact, he was quite alarmed when we tried it on him.) We're just not tub types. We're too project driven to wait for the tub to fill, too busy to sit and soak. We're rinsers rather than soakers, which makes us shower people. We put in a good-sized tiled shower enclosure with a hinged glass door that has magnetic closure strips all around. The shower stall has a large no-slip drain basin to stand on and an adjustable-spray showerhead.

The one-piece toilet bowl was yet another hassle. Because of delays in the renovation, it sat untouched in its sealed carton for several months until it could be installed. When we opened the carton, what did we find? A cracked bowl. The one-piece toilet bowl had become a two-piece toilet bowl. We were not pleased. We were even less pleased when both dealer and manufacturer refused to replace the cracked bowl because "too much time had elapsed since its purchase." We should have opened the carton and checked the bowl at the time of purchase. In the end (no pun intended), we had to buy another toilet bowl or settle for a hole in our bathroom floor. Having tried the hole in the bathroom floor many years before in a Paris bistro, we decided it would not be appropriate in this setting.

Washbasin in third-floor bathroom. No sheep around this one. Mountain sheep and they were put off by all the stairs, can you believe it?

We tried to take comfort in the fact that the toilet bowl was well designed. The sensible bowl shape, a longer standard oval, was, for men, at least, less constricting. Those who have tried both types, vote for the longer oval, hands down. Just don't leave it in the carton too long.

The large medicine cabinet on the wall of the bathroom is cleverly fastened in place with only four screws. This makes it easy to remove the cabinet in order to access all the various venting ducts grouped in a stack in the wall right behind the cabinet. There are a lot of ducts; the furnace, the

The master – and only – bedroom recently.

The master bedroom. This may only be a one-bedroom loft but it has a very lofty bedroom. The fifteen-foot ceiling is a continuation from the living room of the original church ceiling. The light hanging from it is another of the church originals saved and moved. Like the others it's incandescent, but we mounted an extra little halogen spot lamp on it that throws some light on the painting over the window that we also saved. It was one of several in the church under mosaic tile medallions. The large south-facing window, which can be opened, has a two-foot-deep tiled window seat.

The bedroom has a large additional north-facing window cutout up at ceiling level. Also up at ceiling level and at right angles to the cutout is a glass-block window facing west out to the roof deck. It makes for interesting light changes during the day, which vary with the seasons. In the summer, daylight wakes us up early. It's a great way to start the day.

This is probably our most successful room in terms of our minimalist intentions. It's a big space with not too much in it. The queen-sized bed, a "confetti" chair painted in dazzling colours by Colleen, two zed-shaped bent maple plywood night tables and, on the wall facing the bed, a charcoal drawing of a frog serenading a bird. Don't ask. The tiled ledge built out from the block wall at the head of the bed was designed to hide all the wiring, but it also gives us a built-in headboard to put stuff on.

hot water heater, the range exhaust hood, two bathrooms and a powder room are all vented. Richard designed it this way specifically so that if repairs of the ducts were ever required, no walls would have to be torn open.

With the volume to handle it, we were able to incorporate into our lofty mezzanine space design elements that would have been impossible to implement in a conventional home. We had space, for example, for a long, two-entrance, walk-through dressing room. Equipped with racks to hang clothing, and baskets and shelves to store things, the dressing room reduced the need for storage space and furniture in the bedroom. A nine-foot counter has a sink, a well-lit mirror above, and more storage underneath. Another wall has a full-length mirror. Pocket doors at each entrance permit us to close off the dressing room when desired.

CHAPTER 17

OUR NEIGHBOURHOOD

I've held forth at length about the church, the renovation, and the thinking that went into the oversized project, and I hope I've painted a reasonably clear picture. But I'm not so sure that I've painted nearly as clear a picture of the lively area we live in, the downtown neighbourhood that we love so much. Let me, therefore, touch up that picture with a few splashes of colour.

As you will recall, the church that became our loft came available when an innovative developer with a knack for converting non-residential properties into attractive, high-style loft condominiums decided to turn his talents loose on the parish hall six feet to the south of the church proper.

Built in 1950 as a secular extension to the church, the church hall was a substantial masonry structure, pragmatic rather than aesthetic in character, before it fell under the developer's magic touch. First adding a storey to the hall, he then built thirteen handsome, soundly conceived condominium units. Each has a well-designed interior with either a charming patio walkout – land to the south of the hall permitted the

Adding a floor, the church hall today is a handsome thirteen loft condo building that even the visionaries Cyril and Methodius could never have envisioned.

ground-floor units large private gardens at grade – or a bright, sunny deck. Like the people who bought them, no two of these handsome hideaways are alike. Some are on one level, some on two. Some are large, some small. All had been custom finished to the specifications of their respective and, I might add, individualistic owners. Said owners became our next-door neighbours and, in some cases, our good friends. But they aren't our only colourful neighbours. And this isn't the only neighbouring hall.

Just across the street, there's another neighbouring hall with another colourful crew in it. I'm talking about the fire hall, home to a good, reliable group of firefighters who are also great neighbours. Ever considerate of the rest of us, they try not to make too much noise as they go about their noisier-than-average affairs; they are particularly considerate during the night. We quickly got to the point where we hardly hear them. Occasionally, when we do hear them, we'll grin and say, "There go the boys." Even though some of them are girls.

One day, shortly after we'd moved into our

The firehall at night is big and bright. And amazingly quiet. They respect the neighbourhood sleeping patterns and emerge quietly in the evening.

The Urban Loft

part of the church, one of the firefighters came over, introduced himself, and suggested that since ours was not a conventional residence, it might be helpful if a few of the senior firefighters could walk through the premises to get some idea of the layout, should their assistance ever be required. We agreed, and he made an appointment to come back the next day with a group.

The following day, when the emissary returned for the tour, our eyes popped. There was a line-up. He had brought with him not a handful but perhaps two dozen of his colleagues. Apparently when the word got around there was to be a tour, they all wanted to come and have a look.

They seemed much taken with the transformation of the premises; they asked questions and oohed and ahhed in all the right places. And our feelings really weren't hurt when what impressed them most of all was Frank's workshop in our basement set up with all his equipment and power tools. They're good guys; we liked having them visit.

We also liked what they

A few of the interesting shops on the main drag just around the corner from us.

drive. Big and shiny and a great colour. And we loved the fire hall. It would make a great loft. I should have asked if they'd ever consider selling.

Despite all my raving about it, I recognize that the little domain I'm so in love with is not everybody's cup of borscht. Take Frank, our wonderful woodmeister, for example. For nigh on to nine months after we moved into the church, Frank practically lived with us, making us his second home, daily driving in from his other home out in one of those commuter towns just north of Toronto, where he thought everyone should live. For the life of him, Frank

couldn't understand why anyone would choose to live in the city, let alone right downtown, where all the "weirdos" were.

Once when he complained about "all those street people, all those beggars and panhandlers," I suggested to him that the reason we had so many might be because the people in the suburbs and exurbs didn't take their share of unfortunates with them when they moved out to the boonies. Now, we downtowners were stuck with their share and ours.

Frank's unfavourable impression of the inner city may be due to the blinkered view he got of it through his van window as he drove quickly in and out of the area. He often went by a group of our Chinese neighbours, for instance, faithfully doing their graceful early morning tai chi exercises in the nearby park. Not up on the martial arts, Frank couldn't figure out what they were doing. To him, they were more of the "local loonies" that, in his opinion, downtown was dangerously full of. His comments made it pretty clear that if not for his work, he would never have set foot down here.

It seems to me, that if Frank had had the time to get out of his van and take a leisurely walk-around look-around, he might have felt differently about our charming community.

With that in mind, let's do what Frank never had the time to do. Let's try a little experiment that will give you a sense of the neighbourhood. We'll assume you live well away from downtown and don't know our area at all. Now, let's pretend that we've invited you over for coffee. You've arrived by car. When you can't find a parking spot on our street, you park around the corner, a little north of the church. Not

That's our place with the wonderful windows just behind the line of Siberian crab apple trees.

too far to walk. It's a lovely afternoon. Late spring. A chance to look around. You've never been down in this part of the city before. Hey. Check it out.

Little houses mostly. Some detached. A few semis. Lots of row houses. Mostly Victorians. Very narrow lots. Can't be more than twelve feet wide, some of them. And a few truly tiny houses that are really no more than one-room cottages. Had to have been built a long time ago. Well looked after, though, most of them, tidy, recently painted.

They're house proud, most of the people around here, sitting on their porches sunning themselves, hosing down their walks, puttering about in their tiny front gardens with the little fountains and windmills and castles and coloured pebbles. Some are growing corn, some grapes. One even grows tobacco. Quaint, you think, smiling to yourself.

As you approach our corner, your field of vision is slowly taken over by an eighty-foot-long row of tall, stately trees covered in white blossoms. They're the Siberian crab apple trees. They make quite a display in the spring. And they get noticeably taller every year. At the moment, they're maybe fifteen feet high. They can grow as high as forty feet.

And there, in soft focus, through the veil of trees, is your destination, our makeover of the former church. Silent and massive through all the blossoms and the greenery, the renewed building sits silently waiting for you, dominating the block and the view. Still looks sort of church-like, you think. Well, maybe not totally. The trees do make a difference, of course. And the big windows, all that gleaming glass, with the late afternoon light reflecting off them, are really quite unchurchlike. Yet, somehow, the former house of prayer doesn't quite look residential either. It looks . . . well, it looks . . .

Play it safe, you think, grinning. When they greet you at the door, ask for the pastor. Or tell them you've come for the service. That'll get a laugh out of them, if they're not already tired of the joke. (They are. But still . . .)

You cross the street, turn right, and running your hand along the wrought-iron fence's metal rods (old fences bring out the child in all of us), you follow the fence enclosing the front yard and the line of tall trees, admiring the density of the periwinkle ground cover with its little blue flowers and occasionally a few white ones. Abruptly, the row of trees ends. The fence makes a sharp left turn – there's no gate to open – and leads you along a short, broad, welcoming, well-worn, slightly crooked concrete walk – past a burgeoning flower bed to your left and a lacy honey locust tree in a bed of pea gravel on your right – towards the black double entry doors with little stained glass windows in them.

Not much more than a stone's throw away (thankfully), the school my mother went to briefly as a child. Shame she couldn't have gone to school longer. She could have been a contender.

By the doors, just to your right, is the trellis, the handsome trellis, that brightens up the entrance. Notice how it seems to float – blithely almost – in space. And how about the neat light box on the front of it with both the number and the street name on it? (Right. Belt and braces. But with all the hassles with our mail, we weren't taking any chances.) When we turn on the porch light at night, the address lights up, too. The light box has a downturn in it that also casts a little light on the White Lily of the Nile in the attached planter. It replaced a little juniper that didn't make it through the winter, which replaced a bridal wreath spirea that didn't make it through the summer. (This is a high-traffic planter you're looking at.)

Step up onto the concrete pad and you're at the door and

Not all churches become lofts. This former church around the corner from us was converted into a busy community centre and restaurant.

under the safety glass awning. It was made by the same people who made the windows. The button on the doorframe on the right is the doorbell. Press it. Ding-dong. Ding-dong is always followed by Bow-Wow – shades of Pavlov – and scrambling inside the door. That's Satch letting you know (a) that you're on his turf and (b) that he's eagerly waiting for you to enter and pay attention to him or (c) he'll continue to bark at you and make a pest of himself. As far as Satch is concerned, you're here to see him. He's very focused.

The door opens, and there we are, waiting to greet you. Hi. Please, come in. We'll just give the wild beast a dog biscuit and that should shut him up for a while. He's got us well trained.

Now, that I've won you over – I hope – stay with me while I tell you a little more about the area. To my great pleasure, delight, and astonishment, the loft residence, to which happy chance directed us, sits smack in the middle of a neighbourhood that boasts an extraordinary mixture of cultures. The community around our pleasuredome is the most intermingled, most variegated, and most happily heterogeneous community we have ever had the good fortune to live in. This may be a high-density area, yet we have no sense of being crowded.

Every European country is represented here, as is most of Asia, most of Africa, most of Latin America, much of the Caribbean and Polynesia. If they aren't here already, they'll be coming. This is a community for everybody.

There are grand homes here and grubby ones. There are stylish condos and rundown apartment buildings. There are tiny cottages and huge lofts. There are public parks and secret gardens.

The oldest undertaker in the city is in our neck of the 'hood. Handy. You can walk over.

The main drag, just two short blocks from us, is rich with things to buy and see and do and eat. Eateries of every description abound, gourmet dining rooms, specialty coffee houses, endless pizza joints, Italian restaurants, and Indian and Portuguese and Chinese and Japanese and Thai and Vietnamese and Polish and Greek and Czech and Austrian and on and on. From the deepest of dives to the jumpingest of jazz joints, to the hippest of rock palaces, to the swankiest of boîtes, to the funkiest of clubs, the beat goes on.

Just around the corner, there are art galleries galore, and leading-edge design shops, and blocks chock-a-block with high fashion clothing designers; and antique dealers; and retro furniture marts; and born-again clothing shops; and

The Urban Loft

used and rare bookstores; and discount fabric outlets; and gift shops; and designer jewelry shops; and housewares warehouses.

Night and day, there's action on main street and people, all kinds, all shapes, all sizes. The sidewalks are crowded with humanity, the straights and the stiffs and fun folks and funny folks and funky folks. They can be seen strolling, cycling, skating, skateboarding, jogging, walking (or being walked by) their dogs, lugging their groceries, schlepping their kids or themselves. Diverse lifestyles abound, differentiated by their attire, their hairstyles, their skin styles, their tattoos, their punctures and perforations, their jewelry. They're all here: the Boomers, the Gen X-ers, the nerds, the yahoos, the trendy, the stylish, the suits, the vests, the pants, the greens, the grays, the blues, the alternatives, the ethnics, the newcomers, the intruders. And, of course, the interlopers, we two among them.

Speaking for the interlopers – unofficially, of course – I can only say we came here by chance, but we're here to stay because we love it. Gentrification is inevitable, but we hope that it's the gentrification of renewal, gentle and considerate rather than relentless and ugly and overwhelming. We came for community. The old-timers now recognize this, I think, and are happy with the revival and the restoration of their turf. We hope so.

The nearby park is Satch's favourite hangout. That's the local community centre in the background.

The once-upon-a-time rectory is now a downtown residence of distinction.

The Urban Loft

CHAPTER 18

Was It Worth It?

My intense and inordinate interest in living spaces may have come, as I have noted, from having lived in constrained space in my childhood and from having, during my wanderings, occupied a diversity of spaces in a variety of configurations. But there's another reason. And it has to do with the inner me.

I was never a thrill seeker, never a risk taker. Life was risk enough. I didn't need to ride roller coasters. My feet were always on the ground. I never had the urge to fly in a plane. Or outside one. I was never interested in mountain climbing, or rock climbing, or even social climbing. I could barely manage a stepladder. As for high diving – or sky-diving, or bungee jumping, or hot air ballooning, or hang gliding – no thanks. Not my cup of terror. None of that high frisk, high risk, high living for me. I have all the air I need down here on the ground where my feet are.

I'm not into high speed either. What's the rush? I'm in no hurry to go vrooming around town in a sports car or roaring across the countryside on a motorbike, scattering the chickens and disturbing the peace. I have nothing against the chickens or the peace.

Let me add that I don't care for the "multiple" lifestyle either, which requires interaction with crowds. That's why I don't belong to clubs – curling, cricket, country, golf, tennis, lawn bowling, riding, health, whatever.

I also tend to avoid the "duplicate" lifestyle, which requires living in two (or more) places at once. I never had a boat or a cottage or a country place or a farmhouse, or a condo in Florida, or a chalet in the Swiss Alps. The benefits were obvious. No double expense. No double taxes. No double insurance. No double housekeeping. No double gar-

dening. No double repairs. No loading. No unloading. No back. No forth. No driving. No highway. No traffic line-ups. No fumes. No hassle. No wasted time. No stress. No fooling. All this I have gained by hewing to home.

Given all the exclusions with which I've encumbered myself, what place is left to be in, and on, but my home? That may explain why my chief interest and centre of activity, has always been the place in which I live. I've never just resided in a home; I live in it, glory in it, luxuriate in it. For some, home may be where the heart is. For me, home is where everything is.

As I write this, we've been living in our loft for over ten years. That we – the irreverent, the unworshipful – after many years of never having set foot in church, temple, mosque, or religious edifice of any stripe, should end up living in a church has to be one of the great wonders of our time. (Ripley, Guinness, please copy.)

We're still in awe of what's been wrought here; we're amazed by its simplicity, its spirit, its grace, its dignity and its carefree feeling. Rapture may be too strong a word, but sometimes, when the sun is shining, the sky is blue, and the light that comes in the windows and streams through the clerestory is right, the feeling within these walls, within this space, borders on rapture. We don't mind. A little rapture can be beneficial to both heart and mind.

Clearly, loft living isn't for everybody. If you're not an independent, go-your-own-way kind of individual; if you're the sort who chokes on change; if you're the type who thinks the status quo is the only status there is, my advice is to stay put in your comfy, leafy, suburban whatever-it-is and enjoy your driveway and your power mower and your barbecue. If you've chosen to live in a high rise, don't fuss. Just hunker down in your gleaming urban tower and revel in your concierge and your high-speed elevator. Don't let overly enthusiastic people like me talk you into anything that you may hate. Hang in wherever you are. And no hard feelings.

But if you're open to change and new ideas and are intrigued with the concept of loft living (i.e., if you are slightly cuckoo), I'd like to leave you with a few substantive notions about why loft living is working for more and more people.

Among the things I learned from researching, writing, and living this book is the effect on our living spaces and practices of ongoing changes in the traditional family makeup. Industrialization transformed the extended, multi-generational family of yesteryear (or maybe it was yore) into the so-called nuclear family: mother, father, children. (Two generations only per household, please.) This was change number one.

Change number two is still happening, having crept up on us in the years since the Second World War. Over the last half century, in most of the industrialized world, the traditional household of two adults – one male, one female – plus one or more children is no longer the norm. Instead, households of one and two people have become dominant. In this new model, people live alone or with one other person. This shift has been accompanied by a growing movement back into the city core, especially among couples without children, or whose children have moved out. They want to be plugged in to the city and are seeking innovative housing.

Note the word "innovative." Developers, trapped in old market thinking, are not responding with sufficient alacrity. Most of them don't get it. Instead of reworking old buildings innovatively, they're tearing them down. They did this recently, around the corner from us, demolishing two interesting warehouses and replacing them with row houses in a cramped, pseudo-something style that does not improve the block.

Builders haven't yet figured out that the demographic shift is changing the way we look at living space. Childless couples or singles looking for homes have very different spatial requirements than families. There's no need for acoustic and visual privacy, no need for separation of the private and public areas, no need for the traditional upstairs/downstairs splitting of the space.

This new template makes the concept of loft living particularly appropriate. As opposed to the structured spaces of the traditional family home, in which all the domestic rituals revolve around the kids, the loft, with its flexibility, with its openness, is an ideal space for adult households of one and two people.

I stress adult households, because most lofts are not really child friendly. Nonetheless, some families have found that lofts offer a few unexpected advantages. Without caregivers around, and often without spouses to help with child rearing, an open living arrangement ensures more contact and easier supervision of young children. While this is true, the problems of acoustic and visual privacy remain and can be onerous. Loft dwellers with kids will think I'm paranoid. (I am.)

As we're all aware, prior to the industrial revolution, people worked at home, but the dawn of industrialization saw them head out to factories and offices. Now, in the information age, we're coming full circle to working at home. The reintroduction of work into the private home is extensive. According to Terence Riley, twenty million Americans now use their homes as their principal workplaces. That's a heck of a lot of homework.

From personal experience, I can attest that a loft is an ideal home workplace. Colleen and I both work at home and enjoy the relaxed, easygoing ambiance. Where the home office is the principal place of business, the work area may not be limited to a single room but may merge with (i.e., encroach upon) the living space. I'd call this an ideal loft situation, since such merging of work space and living space offers fringe benefits for the worker, such as access to better light, not to mention easy access to the fridge and its contents.

Having said all that, let me now add that my personal rationale for loft living is mainly aesthetic and emotional rather than practical. This book is my attempt to illustrate the benefits of large-scale loft space, space that exists for no other purpose than to be in it, to live in it, to work in it, to walk about in it in constant awe and open-jawed wonder, saying things like, "Oh, boy!" "Oh, wow!" "Yo!" "Hoo Ha!" or whatever it is you say when you like the space you're in.

But don't be fooled by all this joyous burbling. Getting there is a rocky road, fraught with "reno aggro," my pet term for renovation aggravation, which is standard in brave (i.e., foolhardy) endeavours like ours.

Now, of course, our space having evolved into a sort of aesthetic triumph, our misadventures and the reno aggro that accompanied them are fading into misty memory. Since the disbelief and puzzlement of friends have turned into muted approval, and sometimes, outright applause, it's easy for us to strut about and say it was fun. It was. But mostly in hindsight.

So that's it: this com-pletes my inside – and outside – story of a project we thought would never get started and, once started, would never end, an inner-city saga of how an unexpected and unlikely building somehow turned into a singular – not to mention towering – abode, rising beyond our wildest expectations to become the home of our dreams and the source of countless stories that make the recounting of our adventure in church renovation and loft creation an amusing (I hope) as well as a cautionary and instructive tale.

This chronicle of our chronic search and the account of how the church changed hands, looks, and use, can be read as a kind of misguided guide (or a guided miss) on how to achieve – or even, come to think of it, how to avoid – the light-headed lunacy of loft living, based on our own very personal, angst-filled, fear-riddled, cost-fraught, yet oddly exhilarating experience.

In the end and at the end, this is about how our obsessive commitment to our folly overcame all obstacles, rewarding us finally with the high, wide and handsome living space that for so long had been our dream.

Satch claims that he actually wrote this book. But there's no way. He can't even type. You suppose he dictated it to somebody?